THE SCALES DON'T LIE

FIRST PUBLISHED IN MARCH 2015

All rights reserved. No part of this publication may be reproduced, stored in a retrieval system, or transmitted, in any form by any means, electronic, mechanical, photocopying, recording or otherwise, without prior permission of the publisher.

PUBLISHED BY STRIKE-ONE MEDIA LTD
www.strikeonemedia.co.uk

PRINTED IN GREAT BRITAIN BY
THE PRINTING HOUSE, LONDON
www.theprintinghouseuk.co.uk

COPYRIGHT
TERRY KNIGHT

ISBN NUMBER 978-0-9932283-0-8

THE SCALES DON'T LIE

MY MATE TERRY

Matt Hayes and Terry on a film shoot on the River Wye. Matt's been a long-time admirer of Terry's angling exploits.

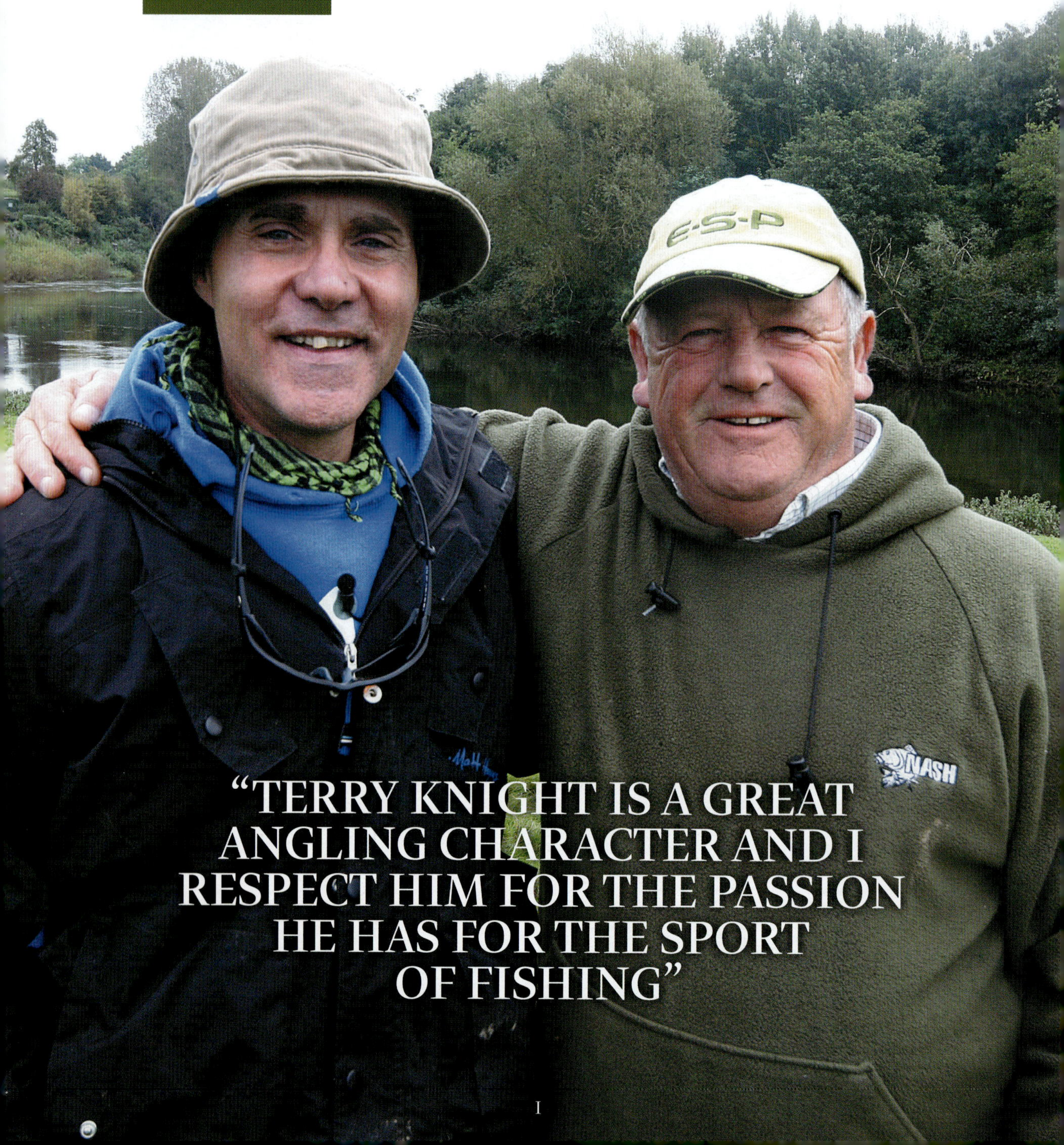

"TERRY KNIGHT IS A GREAT ANGLING CHARACTER AND I RESPECT HIM FOR THE PASSION HE HAS FOR THE SPORT OF FISHING"

THE SCALES DON'T LIE

TERRY KNIGHT
One of angling's true characters

There's a very old saying that claims that if you give a man a fish you feed him for a day; but if give him a fishing rod you feed him for life.

It's a well worn quote that captures the spirit, character and drive of my old friend, Terry Knight, who seems as in love with the sport of angling today as he was when he was catching tiny gudgeon and perch back in the 1950s, on the canals of North West England.

You see, I believe fishing is a gift and in the old days it was handed down through families - often fathers, or in Terry's case, an uncle - and how you embraced that 'gift' shaped your character and life experience.

In the case of Terence Knight, fishing has taken him all over the world, provided an income for his family, not to mention more than a few scrapes and scares. I suppose in those terms, both myself and Knighty share common ground.

As a budding young big fish angler he was an obsessive. A total nut case. No journey was too distant, no effort too extreme as he hunted out the biggest of our freshwater fishes. Those adventures paved the way for some incredible stories and I'm delighted he's found the time to share his unique world.

But this 'warts'n all book' isn't a platform for trumpet-blowing, although the long list of huge specimen fish is certainly worth a fair old toot on the bugle. The project, as he's stated, is a chance to chart his life for his family and loved ones - a first for the Knight name. It should also be an inspiration to us all that expressing yourself through words and pictures isn't just for the select few.

Where 'The Scales Don't Lie' scores over so many fishing books is the photography. Terry and his fishing friends have collated a vast bank of images that are much richer than just traditional 'man holds fish' catch pictures. And what a difference that makes when you thumb through the pages. I've spent many years trying to encourage anglers to look for alternative photographs to chart their fishing history, as it's so much more than just pounds and ounces.

One of my great memories of being on the bank with Terry was during the Great Rod Race TV series when both Mick and myself were really up against it. We needed to catch a catfish to successfully complete the series. We'd got 34 out of 35 species in the bag and had just 24 hours remaining on the clock.

When hope had all but disappeared, Terry invited us to tackle his Burton Mere fishery and under a plume of cigar smoke - the Hamlet cloud is never far away - he put us on the swims and gave us advice on how to tackle the pool. Before sunrise the bite alarm had sounded and we'd snatched victory from the jaws of defeat.

Terry Knight is a great angling character and I respect him for the passion he has for the sport of fishing - he was given a gift and he's certainly made the most of it.

Matt Hayes, February, 2015

ACKNOWEDGEMENTS

THE SCALES DON'T LIE

WITH THANKS TO YOU ALL...

Thanking everyone who has played a part in shaping my life would be a nigh-on impossible job and one that would probably add another chapter to the book! But there are those who are deserving of a special mention.

My wife, Chris, has to be the first - her support, and patience, in 43 years of marriage has been unshakeable. I can't thank her enough.

Angela, my daughter, is the apple of her Dad's eye and I want her to know how extremely proud I am of everything she's achieved. My grandchildren, too, have provided both Chris and I with so much pleasure and I love them dearly.

Catching fish might, at times, seem to take on a ridiculous level of significance, but it's nothing compared to the support given by a loving family.

But, without doubt, it's fishing that has come to define my life. It's shaped who I am, where I go, and who I now call a friend. I've been lucky. I've met some fantastic people over the years, people I may never have ever spoken to if it hadn't been for my Uncle Eddie, the man who sparked the flame 58 years ago.

More recently, and certainly for the past couple of decades, Rich Lee has been my most consistent angling companion. If there's one person I'd pick to sit in a boat with on a rain-soaked, windswept lough in the wilds of Ireland, it would be him. We've shared some special memories and I look forward to more.

Paul Stephenson (Steveo) and Phil Louis are two others who have been constants in some memorable (and not so memorable!) trips over the years. Lads, I raise a pint of the black stuff to you.

Ian Whitehead and Ken Hulme must also take huge credit. They were both instrumental in my early specimen-hunting days and without their wisdom, spirit and love for the challenge, I may not have maintained the fire in my belly that still burns today.

When it came to creating this book, I'd like to thank Steve Partner, Greg Meenehan and Julian Cooke. Great work, boys.

If there's anybody pivotal I've missed I apologise. All my fishing friends - including the fantastic bunch who Chris and I now see on the River Wye for large parts of the year - deserve a mention.

Only space - and my 65-year-old brain - prevent me from doing so.

THE FAMILY

From left to right, Holly, Wayne, Eve, my daughter Angela and my wife, Chris. Fishing has always been a passion, but family comes first.

"CATCHING FISH MIGHT, AT TIMES, SEEM TO TAKE ON A RIDICULOUS LEVEL OF SIGNIFICANCE, BUT IT'S NOTHING COMPARED TO THE SUPPORT OF A LOVING FAMILY"

THE SCALES DON'T LIE
CONTENTS

Introduction **1**

A PIKING OBSESSION
Pike: The King of all Species **5**
Becoming an Addict **11**
Going North of the Border **19**
Glory and the Grief at Blithfield **27**
The Llandegfedd Legend **37**
Tackling the Lakes **43**
The Golden Glow of Ireland **53**
The Mighty Shannon **59**
Life and Near Death on Loug Ree **67**
The Dangers of Lough Derg **73**
A Bonanza on Lough Ramor **79**
Fun and Games on the Upper Shannon **89**
Success on the Secret Water **93**
A New Dawn on the River Wye **105**
My Date with Destiny **115**

A VIEW FROM BOTH SIDES
From Carper to Fishery Boss **121**

BIG FISH FROM BIG WATERS
Chasing the Bream Dream **151**

TARGETING TENCH
In Pursuit of Green Giants **165**

CATFISH
Ultimate Fighting Machines **175**

ASIAN ADVENTURES
The Lake Where Dreams are Made **189**

PERFECT PREDATOR

From a very early age I enjoyed the challenge of trying to catch pike. It was to become a lifelong obsession.

INTRODUCTION

THE SCALES DON'T LIE

WHERE IT ALL BEGAN...

It was at the age of seven that my journey as an angler began, as I pedalled my bike down the narrow country lanes alongside my fishing uncle, Eddie Royal. The dream of catching the monsters in the local stretch of the Shropshire Union Canal raced through my mind and kept my little legs pumping as I powered up and down the lanes.

Little did I know when my quill float disappeared from sight, and the thick tip of my glass fibre rod bounced with promise, that the 8oz perch on the end of my line would spark a 50-year obsession as a fishaholic.

In those early days my fever for fishing grew, and I'd soon become a fixture at Uncle Eddie's local club matches. Too young to delve my hand into the draw bag, I'd tackle up beyond the end peg and dream of one day taking on the seasoned campaigners.

Despite a few wild casts that saw me stick a size 16 forged hook in the nose of the 'lucky end peg draw' and on the next chuck lift his flat cap off his head and send it across the 'cut' to the far bank margin, I soon began to master the tackle and my head was turned by the promise of larger opponents than the gudgeon that seemed to pave the 'Shroppy'.

It was at the age of 12 on a trip to Backford on the same canal that I encountered my first giant. Looking back this was a defining moment that eventually led to me writing my name in the history books in the form of one of the biggest pike ever landed in Britain. Armed with a rod and reel and a tobacco tin of cheap blade spinners, I banked my first ever Esox - a fish that would barely have pushed the spring balance down to 4lb. But such was the ferocity of the take, and the acrobatics of my opponent, that my future was written in less than the 30 seconds it took to crank in the fish. I had to catch bigger pike!

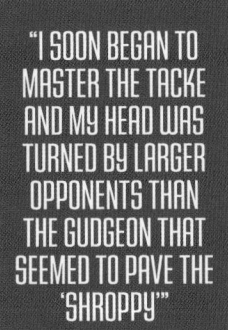

"I SOON BEGAN TO MASTER THE TACKE AND MY HEAD WAS TURNED BY LARGER OPPONENTS THAN THE GUDGEON THAT SEEMED TO PAVE THE 'SHROPPY'"

I became a bit of a loner over the next year or so, often fishing at night, with my mates telling me I had a screw loose. They could not understand what was enjoyable about huddling under an umbrella on a wet, cold night watching my float tip in the beam of a torch light. But I loved every minute of it. They could keep their bottle of Mackeson's and packet of Woodbines.

I had now left school and started work as an apprentice painter and decorator. The first job was to get properly mobile, so as soon as I had scrimped and saved enough money, I purchased my first car - an Austin Cambridge. Those four wheels opened up a new world and allowed me to travel further afield in search of new waters to fish.

After religiously reading the Angling Times every Wednesday it didn't take long to realise that my home county of Cheshire featured regularly. It was far from the wasteland I ➤

INTRODUCTION

THE SCALES DON'T LIE

THE EARLY YEARS

I took my first angling steps on the Shropshire Canal under the watchful eye of Uncle Eddie (above). It was to shape my life in a way I could never have imagined.

feared. By now I had caught most of the UK's indigenous species, but not many of them could be called serious specimens. However, that target was clearly within my grasp.

I was inspired by books and photos of anglers such as Graham Marsden, Roger Harker, Eddie Bibby and Barrie Rickards, to name but a few. Little did I know it at the time, but I would become close friends with some of them in later years.

My first encounter with the 'big league' was on Redesmere, where alongside the late Alan Wilson and rod builder Terry Eustace, I managed to bank a specimen-sized bream.

With my fishing diary now starting to fill with feature fish, I ventured onto other local meres, widening my interest to the pursuit of big bream.

By now I was in my late twenties and had a successful painting and decorating company employing 30 men. That brought with it weekly pressures, but also afforded me the money to start travelling to the Lake District and Scotland in search of the species that first fired my enthusiasm - pike.

The thriving company also allowed me to invest, and I purchased Burton Mere - a water that in time I developed into the North West's first commercial fishery holding specimen carp and catfish. I'd seen how successful Albert Brewer had been at Cuttle Mill and I was sure managed stocked waters for the masses had a future - there must now be over 3,000 commercials in England alone, so it proved to be a shrewd investment.

As Burton flourished, I travelled further afield to try to catch the biggest and the best from all corners of the UK and across three continents.

From Thailand, America, Canada, France, Spain and now my second home - Ireland - it has been a journey full of great memories, monster fish, happiness and a few tears.

Let me share with you the highs and lows of my quest for the biggest...

" I WAS INSPIRED BY BOOKS AND PHOTOS OF ANGLERS SUCH AS GRAHAM MARSDEN, ROGER HARKER, EDDIE BIBBY AND BARRIE RICKARDS "

PIKE PERFECTION

For me, the pike is the ultimate predator. This one came from the River Wye - a venue I've spent more and more time on as the years have gone by.

A PIKING OBSESSION

THE SCALES DON'T LIE

PIKE
THE KING OF ALL SPECIES

Ever since I caught my first pike at the age of 12 from the Shropshire Union Canal, I have been fanatic about the species. And now, 52 years later, nothing has changed. Every winter I still get the same buzz, and even today when my float disappears below the water, or my bobbin drops off my rod rest, my heart always seems to miss a beat in anticipation. To me, they are the perfect predator, and although I still want my next fish to be my biggest, I am never disappointed whether the resultant pike is two or twenty pounds.

For over half a century, I have travelled thousands of miles from one end of the country to the other (as well as Ireland) and I've fished many hundreds of waters in my search of the biggest. Vehicles have been worn out, including one Nissan van that I had especially adapted with cooking facilities and a bed, and I have made many friends, too. Countless pints have also been sunk, mostly in between stories of pike that have been caught or to be caught, and I couldn't guess at how many hours I've spent trying to work out ways to fool what is, to me at least, our finest freshwater species.

There have been lots of changes in pike fishing over the years, with tackle and methods changing beyond all recognition. Long gone are the days of glass rods, Mitchell reels and, in most cases, nylon line, replaced instead by carbon fibre, freespool reels and braid. The choice of hook pattern and size are also now massive, and this has vastly improved the hooking and landing of pike.

Awareness of pike conservation is now, thankfully, on the radar of most anglers and, in general, the era when we would regularly witness idiots dragging them up the bank before kicking them around like footballs is all but over. ➤

THAT MAGIC MOMENT

A beaten pike is ready for the net. I've always been fascinated by the wild nature of pike and the fact they don't have names!

PAGE 5

"EVERY WINTER I STILL GET THE SAME BUZZ, AND EVEN TODAY WHEN MY FLOAT DISAPPEARS BELOW THE SURFACE MY HEART MISSES A BEAT IN ANTICIPATION"

A PIKING OBSESSION
THE SCALES DON'T LIE

IRISH JOY

This 20lb-plus specimen came from Ireland's biggest lough - Corrib. Ireland has been like a second home and I've visited countless times in the last 40 years.

Unfortunately, there still is in some quarters a reluctance to accept the species as part of the natural stock, especially on some of the large loughs in Ireland. What happens on the likes of mighty Corrib, where gill-netting and pike-killing matches still take place, is little short of a scandal. If only they would see sense and realise the importance of balance and diversity, then all anglers would be happy. The fisheries board in the area really need to take a long hard look at themselves - with a little more love for predators, Ireland could be the greatest pike destination in the world.

Luckily, there still is some cracking pike fishing to be found in the Emerald Isle, and there are now a few waters that are being better controlled by local fishing clubs, who are trying hard to protect their stocks for the future.

Over the past 50 years I have seen a lot of changes in the UK, too. In the early days you could, in my view, go almost anywhere and catch fish, whether it be on a canal, river, mere, gravel pit or reservoir. Almost anywhere there was water, there were pike. Sadly, that no longer seems to be the case.

An example of this is on the Cheshire meres.

fish over 30lb have been reported recently. Lochmaben, Loch Lomond and Loch Ken, all waters in Scotland, the latter of which I once enjoyed 33 takes in one day, are also venues that seem to have declined.

In England, Staunton Harold, near Derby, was a great doubles water, but I hear today it does the odd fish, and locals on my favourite River Wye tell me it is nowhere near as good as it used to be. And although I do not get the chance to fish the Norfolk Broads very often, I also believe it's declined in recent years. To me it seems as if this is happening all over the country.

I am not saying that I know all the answers, but I believe fish stocks in all waters do, from time to time, change and some species will thrive at the expense of others.

On the Cheshire meres, the decline of the pike, and other species such as bream, seemed to coincide with the stocking of carp. Maybe because they have such a voracious appetite, the food left available to smaller fish such as roach, rudd and bream has diminished, causing their numbers to go into steep decline. As a consequence, the predators find themselves without a meal. When you look at some of the waters in Ireland, a country where carp still have no real foothold, the silverfish stocks are still thriving and so, in general terms, is the pike population.

However, I can't blame all the problems on the emergence of carp, when cormorants, goosanders and otters are all taking their toll on smaller fish. Collectively, that little lot have had a devastating effect on the sport. Maybe in years to come some of the commercial fisheries may see some of the benefits of stocking pike into their waters and we'll see the species recover.

On the plus side, the past 30 years has seen the emergence of trout water piking, and the results have changed the face of the sport. Never has there been a period of time when so many large fish have been caught, with waters such as Llandegfedd, Blithfield, Chew and many ➤

Most of these venues are only a short distance from where I live, and although they were never renowned for big fish, it was somewhere I could go for a day and I'd always be able to get a few takes. I'd often end up with more than 20 fish in a session. But if I went to these places today, I would be lucky to catch a couple of jacks.

Another example is Rudyard Lake, in Staffordshire. Thirty-five years ago this was one of the best doubles waters in my area, and I caught lots of fish to over 20lb. Since then it has suffered a number of unexplained fish kills and is now a shadow of its former self, although some others pushing weights of pike to record sizes.

If we look at LIandegfedd and Blithfield as two examples, it's important to remember that these trout water pike grow large because they are feeding on T-bone steaks all the time, or the fish equivalent, in trout! They are also supplemented by the vast stocks of coarse fish that already inhabit the waters.

Before being stocked, the trout are fed on high protein trout pellets to ensure they grow speedily, and when the pike eat these fish, this improves their growth rates, too. I used to think that this was a good thing, and if you want predators to grow fast, it probably is, but in the long term, I'm not so sure. It results in the pike becoming obese, just like humans grow obese, and this in turn causes ill health. We all know that seriously fat humans can die young – and maybe this is one of the reasons why trout water pike perish so easily.

There could be many other reasons, of course, one of which is over-fishing. The owners of these trout waters have benefitted massively from the extra revenue generated by the pike fishing, and if they only opened their waters every two years instead of every year this may help to maintain the levels of pike – and also their future income. In my view, if those in charge of record-breaking venue LIandegfedd had done this, they may not have had to shut for five years in the vain hope of the pike population returning.

Another issue that causes me concern is the use of lures. A lot of my predator fishing friends know that I have never been a big lover of the method for catching pike. Now, I'm not about to say for one minute that lure fishing should be banned, because it does, at times, catch a lot of fish, but I have serious concerns about it.

Over the past 20 years, large lures have become very popular in catching pike, and patterns such as twin tail lures and Bulldawgs carry huge hooks that are more suited to catching large saltwater fish that probably end up on the table for food. I've found large rubber lures to be a real nightmare because of the flexibility of the material; it was often the case that the lure would end up in the back of the pike's throat, making unhooking without causing damage very difficult at times.

Some of the large jerkbaits are also a problem, to the point where I won't use them – I'd sooner give up piking. To often I've seen a pike miss on the strike only for the giant hooks to end up in its eyes. I love catching them, but not at the expense of damaging my quarry.

> "I OPENLY ADMIT, ALONG WITH OTHER PIKE ANGLERS AT THE TIME, THAT I WOULD FLOUT THE RULES AND TRANSPORT LIVE FISH TO AND FROM DIFFERENT PLACES"

On my last trip to Blithfield, early in 2013, almost every angler I could see was using very large lures. It seems to be the norm on the venue, but my fishing partner, Richard Lee, and I were catching just as many fish on small jigs, all of which were very easily unhooked and safely returned.

On the thorny issue of livebaits, when I was a lad it was a perfectly legal method on most waters, providing that they were caught from the venue where they were to be used. I openly admit, along with many other pike anglers at the time, that I flouted the rules and transported live fish to and from different places. This is now something I regret. After owning my own water, I now appreciate that my ignorance could have been costly to the welfare of the existing stock.

I was caught using livebaits on a number of occasions and I was even prosecuted, something I am not proud of today. But I remain sure of one thing. If the water I'm fishing allows live fish to be used, I will use them. They are, and always will be, the finest way of catching pike – I just make sure nowadays I abide by the rules.

BEST OF MATES

Rich Lee has been a constant angling companion in recent years. This beauty went 27lb 12oz and came from Iniscarra, whilst the stunning pike (inset) hammered the scales down to 28lb 4oz.

A PIKING OBSESSION
THE SCALES DON'T LIE

BECOMING AN ADDICT

By the '70s, pike fishing in winter had become an obsession. I simply couldn't get enough of my favourite fish. In those early days my long-term angling pals, The Big Fairy (Kev Shore) was still wearing short pants and Ugly (Gary Banks) a twinkle in his Dad's eye.

Almost an hour away from my then home were two waters that I viewed as 'local' - Rudyard Reservoir and Bosley Reservoir - both of which were near Congleton, in Cheshire. At the time, Rudyard was the easier of the two, and with a disused railway track running down the full length of the water, it made winter pike fishing feel as if I were sitting at home in my armchair. Why? Because if the weather was really bad - and believe me a winter in that area of the country is bloody vicious - I could sit in the comfort of the car and watch my drop off indicators through the windows. The number of double-figure pike that were being caught at that time made Rudyard a real gem of a water, and it was certainly the most productive for miles around.

Tackle wise, Terry Eustace T24 glass rods were the most widely used in those days, with carbon fibre non-existent, at least in northerly outposts such as Cheshire! With a test curve of 3.25lb, they were ideal for casting large sea baits such as whole herring and mackerel.

The tackle shops had not got around to selling frozen pike baits, so most of our baits were acquired fresh from local markets and fresh fish suppliers. Unlike today, back then they were plentiful, and in my view fresh sea baits for catching pike far outscore any blast-frozen baits.

It was in those early days on Rudyard that I first met some of the members of the Three Counties Specimen Group, notably Will Gollins and Tony Bolton. They turned out to be two of the nicest guys I have ever met in fishing, being unsung heroes who kept themselves to themselves and got on with the simple art of fishing. Their humility was in stark contrast to some of the other members of the group, and I'll explain more about that later on.

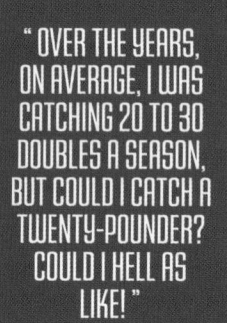
" OVER THE YEARS, ON AVERAGE, I WAS CATCHING 20 TO 30 DOUBLES A SEASON, BUT COULD I CATCH A TWENTY-POUNDER? COULD I HELL AS LIKE!"

Apart from Will, Tony and a few of their friends, it would be rare to see any other pike anglers fishing at Rudyard. Most times I had the place (and the brilliant fishing) to myself. When the weather was good, the fishing was the best you could get anywhere, and I found a full reservoir, winter sunshine, light winds and clear water to provide the very best conditions.

Over the years, on average I was catching 20 to 30 doubles a season, but could I catch a twenty-pounder? Could I hell as like! To me, they were as rare as rocking horse shit, and I genuinely lost count of the number of 19-pounders that I had caught. The annoying thing was, there was an occasional 20lb-plus fish being taken by other anglers, and I couldn't believe I had not had one, especially when I was putting in far more time on ➤

MY FIRST TWENTY

A large sea deadbait accounted for my first 20lb pike - a 21lb 1oz specimen. Bosley Reservoir was a tough nut to crack!

WHAT A FISH!

My first 30lb pike. Bosley once again delivered the goods. Check out my lucky hat - a hat that was to end up at the bottom of Rudyard after blowing off in a gale.

"I REMEMBER LEAVING MY CHAIR AT THE SPEED OF A ROCKET...I KNEW STRAIGHT AWAY IT WAS A BIG FISH"

A PIKING OBSESSION
THE SCALES DON'T LIE

the water than anybody else.

It was in the latter half of the '70s that I decided to split my local pike fishing time between Rudyard and the ultra-hard Bosley Reservoir. I was still chasing my first 20-pounder, and to this day I really don't know why I chose Bosley. I knew little about it, apart from the fact that a few upper doubles had been caught... and that it was rock hard!

But, for some reason Bosley was pulling me like a magnet. For the next couple of winters, together with my piking partner Ian Whitehead, I fished a lot of two- and three-night sessions, often in the worst weather you could imagine. Our bivvy often looked more like an igloo in Alaska than a tent on an English reservoir! Mid-winter on the edge of the Pennines is certainly not for the faint-hearted.

The pike on Bosley turned out to be few and far between, and most fishing sessions finished with a blank. We did manage a few fish to low doubles, our occasional visits to the more obliging Rudyard helping to keep us from going completely mad.

It was at around this time that I joined a group of anglers that called themselves The St Helens Freshwater Study Group. The main man was a guy named Ronnie Pendleton, who truly had fishing at the centre of his heart as he lived for the sport, and for the group.

The Pike Anglers' Club of Great Britain was, back then, nothing like it is today. It had fallen into decline, but new people at the top were working hard to rebuild its reputation, and Ronnie was a big part of that. No better example of this came when he formed the St Helens region of the PAC, and a for while Ronnie and I travelled all over the country to different regions promoting pike fishing with videos and talks. His efforts were rightly rewarded when he was made Pike Angler of the Year.

In the winter of 1977/78 reports began to circulate about the capture of a 28lb pike from Bosley. The place suddenly underwent a huge change. The days when just a few of us hardy souls would tread the banks were replaced by rows of bivvies. Pike, especially big ones, were becoming more and more popular, largely thanks to the efforts of the PAC. But for all of the extra activity and effort, little changed with regards to the amount of fish being caught.

However, the fun on the bank was something else. Ronnie's popularity with the PAC seemed to have upset a few members of The Three Counties Specimen Group, notably a chap called John Roocroft. It soon became obvious to me that a personality clash was developing between Ronnie and John, and my thoughts were soon to prove correct. ➳

> **BELOW RIGHT**
>
> I shared my time between Bosley and Rudyard back in the late 1960s and early 70s. This one, at 23lb 8oz, came from Rudyard.

One day, after having words, the pair ended up rolling around in the grass having a right ding-dong. It ended up with Ronnie sitting on top of John threatening to knock him out! Matters were made even worse a few weeks later when a popular magazine at the time called Coarse Fishermen ran in its regular column, called Snide Rumours and Dirty Lies, a line that went: "Rumour has it that the St Helens mauler has been giving the scrawny Roocroft a good hiding."

The pair of them featured in a number of further editions in the coming months.

Even with all the extra anglers on Bosley, the place was still pulling me like a magnet, and I felt sure that one day it would reward me for all my efforts. On most sessions I was joined by Ronnie and other members of the PAC, and we would spend most of our time on the shallow area of the reservoir, mainly in the hope that any big girls would use this area for their yearly spawning ritual.

Some weekends there were as many as 30 rods lining the bank. Most of them had self-made red drop-off ping-pong balls hanging below the reels. These indicators were brilliant in all sorts of weather, especially in windy conditions, and the only time they dropped off was when a fish pulled the line out of the clip that was attached to the ball. In my view they are the best indicators by a mile, and I still use them.

Week after week we fished the reservoir, waiting for one of the ping-pong balls to drop off, and when one did, which was a rare occurrence, it was usually a jack. But all this was to change on October 8, 1978, at 10am. One of my rods was baited with a whole herring and it was that one that sprang to life when my ping-pong ball dropped to the ground. I remember leaving my chair at the

PICTURED ABOVE

It was heart in the mouth stuff as I played my thirty from Bosley. Looking back, that fish is among the best I've ever caught.

A PIKING OBSESSION
THE SCALES DON'T LIE

speed of a rocket, my heart pounding as I watched line coming off the spool. Very carefully I pulled the hooks home and almost immediately the fish rolled on the surface. I knew straight away that it was my first 'twenty'. I was absolutely delighted when it went 21lb 1oz. But more was to come.

Exactly a week later, in exactly the same spot, I had another take, only this time on a whole mackerel. I couldn't believe it when I took another 'twenty', at 20lb 12oz. I did wonder if it was the same fish, but unfortunately the pictures were inconclusive. I wasn't bothered, anyway; it was another milestone fish from what had been a ball-breaker of a water.

On the days when the wind was too strong I'd head to Rudyard, which was more protected than Bosley. Boy, was it on fire. There were more doubles being caught than I had ever seen from there before, and I was right in the thick of the action. Over a very prolific spell I took 23 doubles, a lot of them in the mid to high teens, and my form continued when I crowned it with a new personal best of 23lb 8oz.

Bosley, though, kept drawing me back. I'm not sure why, because I endured blank after blank, with one 12lb fish caught by one of the St Helens lads the sole highlight in an especially tough period. And to make matters worse, the weather that winter was one of the worst for years. By early January the temperatures around the Bosley area were dropping to -16C and the whole reservoir was well and truly frozen. The snow falls were also very heavy, and at times we couldn't make out where the land finished and the water started.

During what was a long and bleak winter, all we could do was stay at home and wait for the weather to break. My hunger was undiminished - that report of the 28-pounder was always in the back of my mind, and as far as I knew it had not been caught again. Hopefully it was still swimming somewhere in the reservoir, ideally at an even bigger weight. I was convinced that if, and when, I eventually returned to the reservoir, I'd be in with a chance. The swim that had produced the two 'twenties' for me had to be the right area, I just needed to be there to realise my dream.

It wasn't until three days before the end of the season that the ice and snow melted. I was up early on the day that it cleared, my intention to get in the swim that had been my focus during the previous two winters.

When I arrived at the reservoir I was gutted to find a couple of bivvies in the vicinity of the spot that I wanted to fish. When I got bankside I was greeted by some of the members of the Three Counties Specimen group. They had obviously heard about my recent success and had been there for a night or two. My guess was that they were trying to tie up the swims for the few remaining days of the season, a move I could hardly complain about. I had no divine right to fish the swim.

After a few minutes talking to them and weighing up the situation, it soon became obvious to me that they were not actually fishing the swim I had been craving. Their nearest rod, I guessed, was at least 8m away. The name of the member who owned the rod was Mark Swindles, who I had met a few times previously while fishing on Rudyard. I knew him reasonably well, so I asked if he minded me fishing next to him. He assured me it would be fine, and despite sensing there was some reluctance in his voice, I chose to ignore it. I did, after all, have as much right to fish there as any other member.

The one thing I have never disclosed until now was that a few years prior to fishing at Bosley I ➤

> "DURING THAT LONG AND BLEAK WINTER, ALL WE COULD DO WAS STAY AT HOME AND WAIT FOR THE WEATHER TO BREAK. MY HUNGER WAS UNDIMINISHED."

PICTURED ABOVE

A different angle of the Bosley thirty. I love this picture because not only does it show the size, but my expression says it all.

was having one of my many summer walks around the place. The levels at this particular time were very low, and the swim I now craved was almost completely dry. It had exposed a long ditch approximately 40 metres out from the bank running from my right-hand side and making its way down to my left. It was a metre wide and about 5ft deep. Most of us had sussed that there was a feature there, but here it was, every detail on show.

I wandered out to get a better view, and what water was in the ditch was solid with fry - this was clearly an area where pike could lurk, especially given that there was a sharp bend in the trough that made the perfect ambush point. I imprinted the detail in my mind for when the reservoir was full.

Having then fished the swim on many occasions, I came to know it like the back of my hand. Accuracy was vital, and I always wanted my mackerel and herring baits to land either side of the bend in the ditch. Thanks to much practice, I could achieve that with consistency. So, on this particular late-season day I got the baits where I wanted them and sat back to see what would unfold. As I said earlier, waiting for my bobbins to drop off at Bosley was often a long and painful affair. However, call it intuition or just experience, but something told me this was going to be my day.

At around 10am my orange ping pong ball indicator dropped back below my reel. A fish was showing an interest in my whole herring bait. The movement was so slight that if my eyes had not been focussed on my rod, I would probably never have known. In the blink of an eye I was out of my chair and removing the indicator from the line. With the bail arm open, if there was interest from a pike it would feel almost no resistance - I wanted to make it as easy as possible for it to make a mistake.

A minute or so later, the line was running hesitantly through my fingers, indicating that a pike had indeed taken the bait. I deliberated whether to pull the hooks home, my heart missing a beat as I gambled for another second or two, but moments later the fish was now confidently taking line through my fingers and I struck hard into a heavy weight. The rod was bent double as the fish rolled on the surface, and I winced as, with its mouth open, it shook its head violently from side to side, trying to dislodge my hooks.

Thankfully, though, they held in place and I soon guided it over my waiting landing net. It was massive - certainly the biggest pike I had ever seen, and I was over the moon with joy.

On the scales it went 30lb 4oz, setting me a fantastic new personal best. The fact that it was a truly wild predator, caught from the toughest of venues, made it all the sweeter, and it was a time in my life that I will always remember.

I couldn't help but feel for Mark Swindles. He must have felt the same because if I had not arrived that day, he may well have caught it. However, that's fishing, and I have endured my fair share of bad luck in my years as an angler.

I returned to the swim the following year, but I felt the time had gone. The pull of Bosley didn't feel as strong and, deep down, I knew I'd need to head to pastures new if I wanted to catch something bigger. Before I finished with the place I did manage to catch another fish, at 19lb 2oz, but it was on the thin side and not in the best of condition. My fears were that it was the 21lb fish that I had caught the year before.

There was one more interesting day's fishing that I had on Bosley before I moved on. One midweek day I was joined by Will Gollins who, like Mark, was also a member of the Three Counties Specimen Group and someone whom I'd respected for a number of years. We decided we would have a social and fish together for the day, so we spread our six rods over an area of bank 40 metres long, close to where I had caught

> **BOTTOM RIGHT**
>
> Ultimately Bosley produced two twenties and a thirty for me. It was a hard place to fish...but a great venue to learn.

the 30-pounder. They were baited with sea deads and cast different distances from the bank.

It was not long before one of Will's bite indicators fell to the floor. But when he tried to pull the hooks home, the fish rolled on the surface and threw them from its jaws.

As you can imagine, he was gutted. As I've mentioned before, runs on Bosley were very rare, and you couldn't afford to miss any of them. Fifteen to 20 minutes later, the same thing happened again on a different rod. You will find this hard to believe, but over the next three hours we both either caught or lost this fish a further six times. It was unbelievable.

Yes, we had both experienced catching or losing the same pike on other waters before, but never eight times! It only weighed 9lb 8oz, but it had the appetite of a 'thirty' and it only stopped taking our baits when we returned it to the water 200 metres further along the bank!

HEADING TO SCOTLAND

Pike fishing started to gain some momentum in the 1970s and rumours of big fish from Lomond were beginning to circulate.

"LOCH LOMOND WAS MY TARGET WATER. AT 22 MILES LONG AND EIGHT TO 10 MILES WIDE, IT BLEW ME AWAY THE FIRST TIME I SAW IT"

Photography Derek Mcdougall Thinkstock

A PIKING OBSESSION
THE SCALES DON'T LIE

GOING NORTH OF THE BORDER

Back in the '70s, my hunt for big pike pushed me in a northerly direction - the attraction of the many waters in Scotland was too much to resist. Venues such as Loch Ken, and stories of the 72lb pike caught there many years before I was born, really stirred my imagination. Myths they may well have been, but the fire had been lit.

Over a four-year period, I fished many of the lochs around Dumfries and I had lots of predators - it was certainly a good area to hone your fishing skills. I enjoyed many adventures, catching in excess of 20 pike in a day, but unfortunately many of them were jacks. A 'twenty' was a very rare occurrence, but wasn't an impossibility - I can also remember a 'thirty' being taken by an angler from the Rochdale area. I only managed a handful of doubles, which I remember were cracking-looking specimens, and they were always in perfect condition, probably because they had never seen a hook, or pike angler, before.

I couldn't understand why at 14 miles long, Loch Ken failed to yield a good average weight of pike. It certainly wasn't over-fished - you'd be lucky if you ever came across another angler!

But my love affair with the area eventually came to an end when I heard rumours about gill netting and the removal of pike for animal feed. It was the kind of story that touched a nerve in me, and when it comes to pike conservation I can get a little spiky. These rumours were confirmed when I arrived at the New Galloway end of the loch for a weekend session. I was distraught to see gill nets spanning all the way across the shallows to the far bank. Bastards!

I scanned the bank and my eyes focused on a shape in the distance. It was a small boat - the one used to lay the traps. I commandeered the launch and was soon afloat and began to check the contents of the nets. It was quite a tally - the boys at Billingsgate would have been proud. I counted 33 pike from 1lb to 8lb, plus one fish at approximately 18lb.

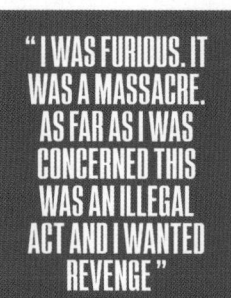

"I WAS FURIOUS. IT WAS A MASSACRE. AS FAR AS I WAS CONCERNED THIS WAS AN ILLEGAL ACT AND I WANTED REVENGE"

I was furious. It was a massacre. As far as I was concerned this was an illegal act and I wanted revenge. On my return to the bank, I sat and watched with a smile on my face as hundreds of cork balls - looking very similar to floats, used to support gill nets - floated down the loch. An act of vandalism? Conservation was striking back.

I had come to the conclusion that Loch Ken had suffered for many years from this practice and it would be highly unlikely that I would catch a really large fish from the venue. In the weeks after the 'cork balls' incident, 'Wanted' posters started to appear in shops and pubs around the area. The ➤

A PIKING OBSESSION
THE SCALES DON'T LIE

police and netsmen wanted help with their enquiries about the sabotage of the nets, and I figured it was now time to move on in my search for a monster pike.

Loch Lomond was my next target water. At 22 miles long and eight to 10 miles wide, it blew me away the first time that I saw it. Balmaha Boatyard - a place made famous by visiting UK pikers - was my first port of call. The yard manager at the time, Jimmy Peirman, was equally as famous as the yard - ranting and raving at everything, and nothing, but once you got to know him, his bark was worse than his bite. In fact he was to become close friends with me and my piking partner at the time, Ken Hulme. Many of the pikers fishing Lomond at that time are still regulars on the bank today, men such as Gordon Burton, John Watson and Paul Davies.

Catching fish from a place as vast and wild as Lomond was never going to be easy. It certainly wasn't a destination for those with a faint heart. At dawn you could be casting into a mill pool, but by breakfast the elements had the power to transform it into the Atlantic in anger. And this could happen in a heartbeat. But with its history of big pike, you always felt there was a chance of a monster.

I didn't know it at the time, but the experiences and lessons I learned while fishing a water the size of Lomond were to be so valuable to my pike fishing future, especially fish location and handling boats on large venues. The power of the winds around Ben Lomond and down to the south end of the loch were always a reminder that pike anglers really know how it feels to be alive.

January 24, 1981, began in a sedate manner. The sun illuminated a glass-like surface and all looked set for a day of leisure. It was one of those dawns that just made you smile: a pikers' morning. However, the fishing had been predictably tough, and despite the winter sun on our backs, Ken and I had failed to get a bite. It was time to head for home.

But as we left Portnellan, with the nose pointed towards Balmaha, it suddenly became a race against the clock, and a fight for our lives. The storm arrived in a matter of minutes, sweeping down the loch with power and pace. It started as a distant murmur, but as it got closer the pounding of the rain and howl of the easterly hit like a sledgehammer. The waves quickly gathered and were crashing into us side-on, flooding the boat. Six and seven foot breakers swamped us. In true 'idiot piker' style, neither of us was wearing a lifejacket. I was convinced that all was lost. We had six miles to go! Not. A. Chance.

> "KEN HELD COURSE FOR OVER AN HOUR AS I WORKED NON-STOP TO BATTLE FOR OUR LIVES..."

I'd crouched low to gain a better centre of gravity when I saw the old empty can of paint in the bottom of the boat. It had been left there ages ago part as a bailer/make-do 'piss pot', but more often a bin for old fag wrappers. I grabbed it so tightly I left nail marks in the dried emulsion, and started to bale water over the side. As fast as I could empty the boat, it would refill.

Ken held course for over an hour as I worked non-stop to battle for our lives, and as we eventually neared Balmaha, I slowly began to win my war against the onslaught. I must have baled that boat more than a thousand times. Thank God for Dulux. Reaching that boatyard was life-saving. And life-changing. Safety afloat has been paramount ever since. Both of us burst out laughing when we finally stepped ashore. It was a bizarre release of emotion but deep down we both knew that the day had been

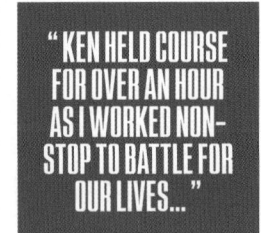

WHAT A SCRAP!

The Lomond pike were, without doubt, the fittest, hardest fighting fish you could ever wish to catch. This 17lb-plus specimen was no exception.

PICTURED
1 Fish to 19lb in a good hit
2 An upper double in the 70s
3 Ian Whitehead with his first twenty from Lomond
4 Two big doubles and a twenty taken in just 10 minutes!

A PIKING OBSESSION
THE SCALES DON'T LIE

far from funny.

I loved Lomond. It was always a challenge, but her fish were stunning. The pike had adapted to their wild environment with perfection, their paddle-like tails gave them thrust and power in the fight. I have never caught any pike that have tested carbon so hard.

Ken and I enjoyed many a good session on Lomond, especially after the first year or two. Once our knowledge and understanding of the loch grew, the numbers of fish caught also improved.

There were vast areas of the loch that were very deep - in some places it plummeted to over 600ft - and trying to catch pike in these areas, if they were there at all, was like looking for a needle in a haystack. We concentrated most of our efforts in some of the many bays around the loch, especially those bays with weed growing in them.

Another good area was the famous Endrick Bank. This bank of silt and sand ran roughly from Balmaha going south for about three miles. It is so shallow in places that you can climb out of the boat and stand up in wellington boots!

There was one area on the drop-off that Ken and I found on our echo sounder that screamed 'pike', the only trouble was it was also smack bang on the salmon anglers' favourite trolling spot. To keep a friendly atmosphere with the game lads, we decided to only fish it when there were no salmon anglers out, or on Sundays, when they were prohibited from fishing.

On one of our many visits to this area, I was fishing on my side of the boat and the pike were really on the feed. In the first couple of hours alone I had taken 12 fish to 14lb, while Ken was pulling his hair out because he hadn't had a single run.

In the name of good boat relations, I suggested to Ken that we swap the rods over so that he could have a chance to catch a few fish. He didn't need a second invite! Within minutes he had two 'twenties' in the boat. I was speechless. To make matters worse, a week later, fishing the same spot, Ken took his Lomond personal best of 28lb 3oz... and I blanked.

Probably the best-known, and most consistent, pike-catching area on Lomond was Cronin Bay, as well as the boat buoys around Balmaha Boatyard. This part of the loch was relatively shallow compared to the rest of the water, and at times there was plenty of weed in the back bays, which was perfect for when the pike wanted to spawn. The secret was to be in, or near, the bays when the fish arrived en masse for spawning.

> "THIS WAS BY FAR THE BEST TIME ON LOMOND...I WAS ONE OF THE LUCKY ONES TO ENJOY THE EXPERIENCE"

This was by far the best time on Lomond. There were many big hits enjoyed by pike anglers at this time, and I was one of those lucky ones to enjoy this experience.

It all started early one morning. Ken and I had by now purchased a second boat, and we were heading towards Cronin Bay. We were convinced that we were the first boats out and were looking forward to having the back of the bay to ourselves. However, on our arrival we were gutted to find two anglers had beaten us to it, and we had to settle for the area just outside the bay entrance.

After two hours, we had only managed a couple of jacks, but to make matters worse, the boat in the bay was hammering the pike. It was carnage in there. Every time I looked up a fish was being brought on board. I had their tally at about 20 pike, although they seemed to be mainly on the small side, but we knew from experience at this time of the year the bigger specimens would not be too far away - it was only a matter of ➻ time.

A PIKING OBSESSION
THE SCALES DON'T LIE

WHAT A HIT!
A 26lb 8oz fish led what was probably, at the time, the best day's piking I'd ever had. I had between 40 and 50 fish in a morning.

I'd just settled back for a snooze when I heard the distant clink of an anchor chain banging against the side of a boat. I turned round and realised they were moving off the fish. As they chugged past they declared that the bay only had tiny pike in it and they were wasting their prime livebaits on catching them. I bid them 'good luck' and was into their spot like a rat up a drain pipe.

The next four hours could only be described as sensational. The action started from the very first cast and even though I started fishing with three rods, I was soon down to one. The baits were being taken as soon as they hit the water!

On the odd occasion when I managed to fish a second rod, I would often end up with two fish on at the same time. On one of these rare moments with two rods, I managed to land two twenties, one at 22lb and the other at 26lb 8oz. They were the only twenties of the session - I was catching doubles for fun and, believe it or not, they were all being taken on sea baits. In that sensational four hours I had lost an accurate account of the amount of fish I had caught, but it was somewhere between 40 and 50 fish, the smallest being about 8lb.

Ken, who had been fishing no more than 30 metres away in his boat, also had a few doubles but nowhere near the amount I had boated. It was just one of those strange things that often happen in fishing - it was just my day.

The session only came to end when I landed the smallest pike of the day. One of my size 6 trebles was outside of the fish's mouth and I lost control of it in the bottom of the boat as it slid off my unhooking mat. This resulted in the loose hook - the one with the barb on it - finding its way into my finger.

After 15 minutes of Ken unsuccessfully

trying to remove it, the pain was becoming unbearable, much to the delight of my partner, who had one eye on my swim. A hospital visit was now a certainty. On my arrival at the local A&E department, the doctor in charge requested that I hold the pair of forceps that he had fixed to the treble hook with my other hand while he cleaned around the wound.

I was contemplating some pain relief when he suddenly grasped the forceps and yanked the hook out. I must have leapt three feet in the air with pain and shock. Hardly expert surgery, but at least it was over.

I wasn't surprised when I returned to Cronin to find that all the anglers who had been fishing from the bank near where I'd been catching had surrounded my hot spot. I wasn't bothered - I'd had one of my best day's pike fishing ever, and a new Lomond personal best. I would have probably done the same.

PICTURED ABOVE
The business end of a big pike. No matter how many I catch, I never tire of fishing for them.

THE FIRST BOAT
The vessel I shared with Ken Hulme. It would have been impossible to fish Lomond without it.

A PIKING OBSESSION

THE SCALES DON'T LIE

GLORY & GRIEF AT BLITHFIELD

In the late '70s and early '80s I was very fortunate to hear about the pike fishing on Blithfield Reservoir, in Staffordshire. I didn't know it at the time, but this place was to have a massive impact on my fishing career, and nearly 35 years later I'm still fishing there on a regular basis. In those early years, it provided me with what I can only describe as the finest pike fishing I had ever seen or been part of. It was simply awesome, and it was always a real privilege for me to be fishing there. However, it didn't start like that…

My first half dozen or so adventures were extremely disappointing. I couldn't catch a pike to save my life, and I ended up getting really frustrated because every time I

A PLACE IN HISTORY

Blithfield Reservoir. I was to enjoy some superb days and some dark ones, too.

A PIKING OBSESSION
THE SCALES DON'T LIE

arrived at the reservoir, what had now become the prime swims were always taken by other anglers.

The swims on The Duckley's and Watery Lane are two of the most famous pike-catching areas on the reservoir, and they are located either side of the road that bisects Blithfield. In those days, in the main it was bank fishing only, and if you weren't fortunate enough to be in these swims, you felt as though you might as well go home. Pike being caught from other areas of the reservoir was very rare, at least while I was there.

The rules strictly prohibited the use of livebaits, with sea baits or lures the only permitted way to catch the pike. But it soon became obvious to me that not only was I fishing the wrong areas, but also that sea baits were a waste of time. After some discrete investigations I found out that lures were catching a few pike, but that the bulk were falling to illegal livebaiting. For me to sit there and blank while others broke the rules was too much for me to bear, so I reluctantly decided to go down the livebait route.

As I have said earlier in this book, I have no problem with the practise of using live fish as bait; after all, I grew up in a time when it was the normal and accepted way of catching pike. Taking it away from my fishing was like taking lead shot away from a shooter and asking them to use rubber bullets instead. I don't like breaking rules of any kind, but it was a widespread practise at the time on Blithfield and I felt that I had to join in just to compete on a level footing.

> "FOR ME TO SIT AND BLANK WHEN OTHERS BROKE THE RULES WAS TOO MUCH TO BEAR, SO I RELUCTANTLY WENT DOWN THE LIVEBAIT ROUTE..."

On my next trip to Blithfield I arrived early enough to be first in the queue for the hotspots. Piking was allowed only at weekends, so I arrived late on the Friday evening. After I had parked my car I made my way down in the dark to my preferred swim at the side of the road. But as I approached it, I was stunned to find somebody else's rod rests already in the swim! I got the fright of my life when a dark shape suddenly appeared at my side.

"Too late, Terry, I've beaten you to it," a voice whispered in my ear.

I should have known that if anybody was going to get there before me, it would have to be Neville Fickling. However, even with Nev being in my intended swim, it didn't bother me too much because all of the first few spots either side of the bridge were constantly producing pike.

The next morning finally arrived and my two rods were soon out in the water. One was baited with a whole mackerel, the other with a six-inch live roach. Action on the ➤

PICTURED ABOVE
A bitterly cold day on Blithfield Reservoir. Lure fishing in freezing conditions is hard work!

MOODY BLITHFIELD

It can be a tough water when conditions are wrong. I'm no great fan of lures - especially big ones - but they do provide an alternative method.

latter was almost immediate, with a pike of 19lb (my first pike from Blithfield) the first of a day that provided consistent sport. I went on to land a further six fish to 23lb, all taken on live roach, while I didn't have a single run on the deadbait.

On that trip I realised the full extent of the illegal livebaiting that was going on. Almost all of the pikers on the bank I was fishing were using them, and the few that weren't were catching nothing. I have to say that I wasn't happy using them. I was continually looking over my shoulder in case of any bailiff activity, and it was doing my head in, together with the thought of being caught.

Over the coming weeks I continued to use livebaits, and never saw a bailiff checking anybody's fishing tackle made me feel a bit more relaxed about it. Maybe I was becoming too complacent. Livebaiting continued to produce the goods and I was catching plenty of pike. I was enjoying every minute of it, too, but little did I know that disaster lay just around the corner.

One morning, after casting my baits into the reservoir I was sitting under my umbrella minding my own business when a young lad casting his Toby came too close to my rods. Before I had a chance to move him on, he had cast over my livebait rod and caught the line. I asked him not to pull any more and explained that I would untangle the mess he had caused. I remember looking up the bank in both directions to make sure there were no bailiffs approaching and when it seemed all clear, I set about untangling the lines. My livebait was swimming happily around my feet while I got on with the job in hand when suddenly

> **PICTURED ABOVE**
>
> A superbly-conditioned 24-pounder on a trolled herring. When Blithfield's right, it remains a great water.

PAGE 31

A PIKING OBSESSION
THE SCALES DON'T LIE

there was a tap on my shoulder.

"Is that a livebait you are using, Sir?" asked the bailiff, knowing full well that's exactly what it was.

To say I was gutted would be an understatement. I had been caught red-handed and for the first time in my life I was speechless. I stood there, like a chastened schoolboy, with my head down in shame as I was read the riot act. I couldn't defend myself. I had taken a chance and been caught - it was as simple as that.

"Can you now pack up and leave the water, please, Sir," were his final words to me.

The drive home felt like the longest journey I had ever made. I couldn't help but think of the people I had let down, and how my reputation would take a serious dent. Yes, it was my fault, but I had been unlucky. That young lad could so easily have caught anybody's line, and at the time I wished he had. I didn't realise it then, but the consequences of my actions would haunt me for years to come. It certainly cost me the chance to enjoy some of the best pike fishing that this country had

PICTURED ABOVE
Taking on big reservoirs afloat is not for the faint-hearted. But I still love boat fishing, no matter how rough the conditions.

THE RACE IS ON!
The mad morning rush begins! It's always pandemonium when the boats head out in search of the most popular marks.

PAGE 32

A PIKING OBSESSION
THE SCALES DON'T LIE

ever seen, and in my absence Blithfield went on to produce numerous huge pike to more than 40lb.

It was many years later before I had the chance to return. A change of management had taken place, and John Davey, who I had known for many years, was now running the winter pike fishing events. I owe him a great deal of thanks for his understanding and willingness to allow my return. I vowed I would not let him down.

My first trip back was in 2007, when I was joined by Rich Lee for a two-day session. Little had altered in the years when I'd been away, bar the surrounding trees growing taller, and it felt great to be back. But while Blithfield may have looked the same, there had been one significant change - the introduction of boat fishing. As far as I was concerned, this was a massive step forward because not only did it open the door to many more methods, but also it opened up new areas, too.

I hadn't boat-fished on Blithfield before, and Rich had never been on the venue, so we decided trolling herrings on our electric motor would be our best approach. With the help of our fish-finder, we figured that this combination would be the quickest way to assess the different areas and depths of the reservoir.

It turned out to be a good decision. Over

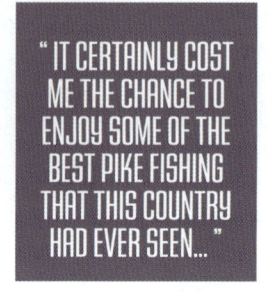

> "IT CERTAINLY COST ME THE CHANCE TO ENJOY SOME OF THE BEST PIKE FISHING THAT THIS COUNTRY HAD EVER SEEN..."

BLITHFIELD BEGINNINGS
Landing a twenty-pounder in the early days when bank fishing was allowed.

PAGE 33

WHAT A START!

Rich Lee with a 27-pounder caught within minutes of casting out on his first trip to Blithfield. Jammy sod!

GET ON THE JIGS!

This 27lb 12oz beauty came on a freezing cold day while the rest of the anglers on the reservoir blanked. It came with another pike, this one at 22lb 9oz.

two days we caught on average one fish every hour, with a couple of jacks, a lot of doubles and a cracking fish of 27lb-plus to Rich. My best on that trip went 19lb 6oz - not a monster, but a great way to mark my return.

Over the next couple of years the fishing was, in the main, good and we managed to get to most of the open day sessions, during which it was rare for neither Rich nor me not

PICTURED ABOVE
You don't need big lures to catch big fish. One of a similar size accounted for the 27lb 12oz pike pictured at the top of the page.

to catch a 'twenty' or two. I even managed to push the weight of my best fish from there up to 26lb 4oz.

On of the most memorable days was in January 2012. The weather certainly didn't suggest that it was going to be a good trip, as it was probably the coldest conditions that we had ever experienced on Blithfield. The thermometer showed -7 Centigrade at midday, and there was a white covering from overnight snow, so we naturally expected the fishing to be slow.

Rich and I decided that we'd have a change of tactics and try our luck at catching some of the large perch that also inhabit Blithfield. This we would do by using a method called jigging. For those of you who have never tried it, join the club. It was about to be my first experience.

Rich had some limited knowledge and I was relying on him to be my tutor. The gear we

A PIKING OBSESSION
THE SCALES DON'T LIE

were using was as follows: a 6ft 6ins multi-purpose predator rod; a very small reel loaded with 15lb braid; and small jigs up to two inches long with interchangeable leads. Rich explained to me that the idea is to lower the jig to the bottom of the reservoir, then lift and drop it just off bottom. The action resembles a small fish in distress, encouraging any predator to home in and attack it.

Right from the off, the action we experienced that day was incredible. With the use of our drogue to slow the boat down in the light wind, we were moving from one side of the reservoir to the other, and when we drifted over a shoal of perch, we would often experience multiple hits on the jigs.

The final tally of perch for the day was well in excess of 20, with many of them between 2lb and 3lb. But the real bonus was that I was to be the one with the golden bollocks this time, taking one pike of 22lb 9oz and my best fish from Blithfield at 27lb 12oz. All hail the jigs!

Over the past few years, Rich and I have thoroughly enjoyed our trips to Blithfield and we would not have missed them for the World. However, we felt dark clouds were again on the horizon. Pike numbers began to drop off and, as I said earlier in the book, I fear that what has happened on other trout waters is now happening on Blithfield. I can only plead with the present owners to shut the place down before it's too late, to give the pike a rest and give them a chance to replenish.

Financially, the owners of most trout waters have done very well out of the extra income from pike anglers, but it's now time to protect future revenue by showing some foresight. If not, a chapter in pike fishing history will come to an end.

> **PICTURED BELOW**
> Time to head for home. The sun sets after another day on Blithfield.

PART OF HISTORY

My best at Llandegfedd was this one at 32lb. It came on a morning when I lost several others of a similar size.

A PIKING OBSESSION

THE SCALES DON'T LIE

THE LLANDEGFEDD LEGEND

PAGE 38

A PIKING OBSESSION
THE SCALES DON'T LIE

My LIandegfedd experience was something very special, although my pike captures weren't fantastic from there. Steveo, on the other hand, took fish that would stand up against the very best. It's highly unlikely in my lifetime that the pair of us will ever have the chance to fish a water of that calibre again. I feel very privileged to have been there when so many large fish were being caught. The winters of 1988 to 1992 were awesome, and at the time LIandegfedd was regarded as the best pike water in angling history.

On our very first day there, Steveo and I were fishing plugs outside the small bay on the North Bank and we were quickly off the mark, catching fish of up to 12lb - not the monsters we wanted, but it was a good start.

But the pike suddenly went off the feed, so in desperation for a bit of fun, Steveo decided to try a small Mepps spinner, and after a few casts his rod hooped over. I went immediately for the landing net, but Stevo called for calm.

"It's only a jack," he said, nonchalantly.

However, I had a better view of the fish and as I slid the landing net under it I could see it was massive. As the predator lay on the unhooking mat in the bottom of the boat, Steveo sat motionless. He couldn't seem to find any words whatsoever. She had an immense frame, with a tiny spinner hanging from her scissors that looked quite ridiculous. On the scales she went 38lb, and at the time was the biggest pike either of us had ever seen.

The joy was not to last very long, though. As we went to return the pike it soon became obvious that, for whatever reason, it was struggling to swim away. We spent the next three hours doing everything we could to keep her upright, to aid her recovery, but eventually we had to move on. All we could do was leave her in the correct position and pray that she would find the strength to swim away. As we later discovered, this problem of returning fish was being experienced by most of the anglers that had caught pike on that specific day.

Over the next few years, my time on LIandegfedd was often cut short due to business commitments. During my absence there were a number of very big fish boated. Stuart Gillham had a fish of 44lb, Carl Garratt one of 44lb 8oz and Brian Ingram took a 43lb 2oz specimen. Meanwhile, first Gareth Edwards (45lb 6oz) and then Roy Lewis (46lb 13oz) went on to set British records - the latter weight remaining the benchmark today.

In my absence, Steveo was also having the time of his life. He would snap up any available dates he was offered, often travelling the long distance from the Wirral for a single day's fishing, that's how good the place was during that period.

By the time I returned to the banks of LIandegfedd, Steveo had taken 16 'twenties' and another five 'thirties'. I would often ask him whether anglers were still having problems when returning the fish, and he'd tell me that although not all the pike struggled, a big percentage had issues. That fact never sat easily with me, and inevitably the captures went steadily downhill.

My most memorable day there was in October 1992, when Steveo and I were in one boat and

> **PICTURED BELOW**
> The pike fishing on Llandegfedd Reservoir made history. Only Chew Valley has matched its incredible results.

PAGE 39

WHAT A FISH!

Paul Stephenson did very well at Llandegfedd. This one went 36lb 6oz and came from the North Bank to a spinner bait.

A PIKING OBSESSION
THE SCALES DON'T LIE

our friends, Phil Lewis and Steve Openshaw, were afloat alongside us. We were anchored in 52ft of water, just off the North Bank, and within minutes we could see large fish breaking the surface, swirling at trout.

However, I was to endure a morning that was packed with rotten luck. Three very large pike were lost on a black and yellow spinnerbait, and during this era on Llandegfedd, you didn't want to miss a single take, as these might have been record-breakers.

To make matters worse, I was then retrieving my spinnerbait when my rod jerked in my hand. I struck, only to miss it. As I threw my hands in the air, Steveo cast at the swirl and hooked up... it weighed 32lb 6oz and was his seventh 'thirty'. You just couldn't make it up.

Meanwhile, the Lewis and Openshaw partnership were also enjoying themselves, with Phil taking a 30lb 8oz pike and Steve one at 28lb 4oz. I took time out to have a brew and establish whether I was fishing like an idiot or suffering terrible fortune. I sharpened my trebles and decided it was the latter.

Refocused and refreshed, I had only made two casts when my lure rod kicked and bucked, signalling that a fish was on. I'd like to pretend that the fight was full of drama and intensity, but it was all rather sedate. Steveo soon slipped the net under a very big girl, and on the scales she weighed 32lb. I felt the relief disappear from my bristling shoulders. A new personal best had ended probably the worst few hours I'd ever experienced at a water.

To try to help the pike recover, we'd started to retain them for short periods in sacks, and this seemed to help a little. It also meant that with three fish caught at the same time, we could get a unique picture - a hat-trick of thirties in the same shot. Thankfully, on this occasion all of the pike swam away to fight another day.

As we predicted over the next year, the quantity of fish landed nose-dived, and for us it was largely uneventful. But during our time on Llandegfedd we'd enjoyed the sport of dreams and been part of an era that had re-written pike fishing history.

> **PICTURED BELOW**
> Three mates, three thirties. From the left, Phil Lewis with a 30lb 8oz fish, yours truly with one of 32lb and Steveo with his at 32lb 6oz.

ANOTHER KIPPER!

Paul, aka Steveo, with another of his thirties, this time at 35lb 11oz. He enjoyed a purple patch on the water.

THE BIG GIRL

Steveo's best fish from Llandegfedd was this 38-pounder. Looking back, I'm grateful we had a chance to be part of pike fishing history.

WILD AND WONDERFUL

I was always looking for new adventures, and the Lakes offered just that. This was the quality of the fish that was on offer.

A PIKING OBSESSION

THE SCALES DON'T LIE

TACKLING THE LAKES

By the late '80s and early '90s I'd switched my attention in search of big pike to the Lake District. At the time little was known about the vast waters in the area, apart from the fact that most of them did hold some pike, although accurate reports rarely appeared in the press.

What little information I did manage to find was on famous venues such as Windermere and Coniston Water, and it suggested that they would be very difficult to fish for a variety of reasons. Weather conditions and the removal of pike were issues on Coniston, and speedboat activity on both, but especially Windermere, meant significant hurdles to overcome. Hurdles, I decided, that were simply too big to take

PAGE 44

A PIKING OBSESSION
THE SCALES DON'T LIE

on at the time.

Therefore, I decided my time would be better spent on the smaller waters such as Bassenthwaite. I discovered, through a friend of mine, that the water had produced fish in excess of 30lb in recent years, the other attraction being that very few anglers fished it at all. As I like a challenge, this became the obvious place to target in my pursuit of big pike.

On most of my fishing trips to Bassenthwaite I was joined by my long-time piking friend Paul Stephenson, otherwise known as 'Steveo'. Over four to five winters we were never off the place - we simply loved every minute of it. The fishing was very hard at times, but the scenery, the locals and, in particular, the local pub, which we nicknamed the 'Six Tits' (a mum and her two daughters ran the place) always made it an adventure. We were fishing on Bassenthwaite that much, we even joined the 'Six Tits' darts team - it really was a great pub in which to spend the cold winter nights.

The lake is very open, approximately four miles long and half-a-mile wide, with a lot of varying depths down to about 50ft and more in places. The wind often was a nightmare - it used to howl around the local fells and down the lake, causing the waves to swell up to five feet in height. In these extreme conditions, most of our fishing was done from the banks in deep water, but when the weather was good, the use of my small six-foot plastic boat to take the baits out beyond casting range was invaluable.

However, this method of presenting our baits at distance did at times have hidden dangers, and over confidence in a small boat can lead to disaster. On one occasion, I was rowing the boat back towards the bank from a distance of approximately 200 metres when I decided to stand up to look through the gin-clear water to the bottom of the lake. I did not see a very large boulder that lay just under the surface of the water until it was too late, and as I hit it I fell out of the boat and found myself standing on the tips of my toes.

I was just about able to keep my mouth above water to avoid drowning. Luckily for me, the bottom of the lake was fairly firm, and I managed to make my way slowly back to the bank, without the boat, which by now had drifted further down the lake with Steveo in hot pursuit.

In those days, livebaiting was not as frowned upon as it is today, so our first choice of attack was always live rainbow trout, which at the time we could purchase from most trout farms. So our conscience was clear, too. As far as we were concerned, purchasing and transferring fish in this way was completely acceptable, because all trout farms were regularly tested for any diseases before stocking. This was the late '80s, and the rules - and awareness - weren't what they are today.

Over a four-year period, Steveo and I, together with many of our friends, caught numerous pike of varying sizes, and a few ➤

> **PICTURED BELOW LEFT**
>
> Mean and moody, the Lakes provided a superb challenge. I enjoyed every minute.

BEST OF BASSENTHWAITE

Caught in 50ft of water, this 24lb 8oz pike was the heaviest I had from Bassenthwaite.

PAGE 46

PICTURED

1 Unhooking a 24-pounder with Steveo
2 My best from the lakes - a 29lb 3oz fish from Esthwaite
3 Another Esthwaite biggie - this one went 26lb

A PIKING OBSESSION
THE SCALES DON'T LIE

of them went over 20lb. But a 'twenty' was a rare fish, and during our time on Bassenthwaite we never heard or saw any specimens bigger than the 24lb 9oz pike I took on trout paternostered livebait from a depth of 54ft.

All good things unfortunately come to an end, and my Bassenthwaite experience was no exception. I didn't know it at the time, but my first run-in with the authorities was just around the corner. On my last day's fishing there the weather was the most diabolical you could imagine - 80 mile per hour gusts and torrential rain. I had tucked myself away in a quiet corner of the lake where the wind was blowing from the back of me, and was so strong that a simple cast sent my baits 70 yards or more!

It was while I was sitting under my brolly, questioning my sanity, that two NRA bailiffs arrived. They asked me to produce my fishing licence, and while they were checking the paperwork I asked them what they were doing out in such foul weather. The tone of their reply was very aggressive, and I wished I'd never asked.

They told me they wouldn't normally be bothering with coarse anglers in these conditions, but they had received reports recently of salmon poaching activity in the mouth of the river, which was a short distance from where I was fishing, and could I keep my eyes open. I agreed, but any sense of an amicable conversation came to an abrupt end.

They spotted I had a third rod in the margins, a feeder set-up that I'd cast out through boredom from time to time.

"Sir," one said calmly, "you are fishing more rods than is allowed. What's more, why are there two rudd swimming in that bucket?"

I'd lost it by now.

"Because I brought them with me you a***hole," was my stupid response.

Two months later I was fined over £100. Technically, I deserved it. I'd broken more than one rule, and the two NRA lads were just doing their job. It was another lesson learned.

Esthwaite Water, also in the Lake District, had been on my radar for some time. Steveo and I had heard on a number of occasions about one or two decent-sized pike being caught accidently by trout anglers, and as we knew it was stocked regularly with rainbows. It just had to be worth a go. Little did we know at the time, but Esthwaite would turn out to be a real gem of water. At last us Northerners had a venue that could compete with places such as Bough Beech down South.

We were lucky. During that late '80s and early '90s it was at its best. The place was full of large predators that had almost certainly benefited from neglect and the regular stocking of protein-rich food.

From the very first day that Steveo and I fished there, we were catching fish to over 20lb, and they were all on the fat side. Over the next few years we had some of the ➺

PICTURED ABOVE
Fighting a low twenty on Bassenthwaite. Back then, the pike were barely fished for and fought very hard.

PAGE 48

A PIKING OBSESSION
THE SCALES DON'T LIE

> "STEVEO ALSO HAD THE FIRST FISH OVER 30LB THAT WE KNEW OF, A FAT PIG WEIGHING 30LB 4OZ"

PICTURED ABOVE

Paul Stephenson, aka Steveo, with his 30lb 4oz Esthwaite giant. It was obese with spawn but that couldn't be helped.

best pike fishing of our lives - and the cherry on the cake was that we virtually had the place to ourselves! The lake was somewhere near 300 acres, which gave us lots of scope for boat fishing, and there was also good bank fishing when the weather was poor. Plus, another great angling edge about Esthwaite was the fact that we were allowed to purchase small quantities of live trout for bait. Like I said, it really was a golden place and a golden period.

Trolling livebaits from the back of the boat and the use of fish finders to chart depths was the method that we found the best. The bottom of the lake had many features, and this approach allowed us to work them with more accuracy. It helped us a lot in our search for ambush spots where pike would be lying in wait to feed on any unsuspecting prey.

Over the next couple of winters I cannot remember any blank days on Esthwaite. We were catching pike for fun, and a lot of them were over 20lb. I was on cloud nine, having caught seven fish over 25lb, the best going 29lb 3oz. Steveo was also doing well and increasing his number of twenties. He had the first fish over 30lb that we knew of, a fat pig weighing 30lb 4oz. If truth be told, in a natural stocking environment it would have been nearer twenty.

By now, word had circulated about how good the pike fishing was, and inevitably more predator hunters began to arrive. We didn't necessarily view this as a bad thing at the time, because the increase in revenue to the owners, who at the time wanted all pike killed to safeguard trout numbers, would prove to be a persuasive argument. Why kill off a growing cash stream? Steveo and I now felt we had a water with a great future that would go on and become even better.

With the increased numbers of pikers now fishing Esthwaite, and with more fish being landed, its true potential was beginning to shine. And shine it did, with more 30lb fish photographed and publicised. Steveo took another one at 32lb, a friend of mine at the time, Chris Bigger, from Liverpool, had one also at 32lb, Tony Cookney, from Windermere, boated a beauty at 34lb 12oz, and Dave Kelbrick soon followed with one at 36lb 6oz. But the largest fish I know about was a whopper at 37lb-plus to Dave Lumb. The size of the fish were certainly on the up.

> **PICTURED ABOVE**
>
> A 26-pounder from Esthwaite. At the time, it was a prolific water but, like most pike venues, it didn't last.

At that time the season was short. Esthwaite was only open from the beginning of November through to the end of February, and I have to say this truncated window was a great idea because it gave the pike a period of time to recuperate and pile on the pounds. We all know the dangers from over-fishing for the species – they simply don't like it.

So you can imagine how I felt when I heard the owners had given permission for the Lure Society to fish for a number of days on the place in the middle of summer. I was distraught. I tried everything I could to change their minds, on the basis that a short-term cash injection was short-sighted. Yes, they'd make extra money from the pike community – but at a potentially disastrous longer term cost.

A PIKING OBSESSION

THE SCALES DON'T LIE

I pointed out numerous waters where similar activities had taken place, and described the often dire consequences. As I said earlier, lures do catch a lot of pike, especially in the warmer weather, but at a heavy price.

I find it very hard to understand the Lure Society. They are supposed to be pike lovers, yet they persist in their pursuit of them with oversized lure patterns that have the potential to cause significant damage. They also fish for them during the summer, when the pike are at their most vulnerable. In my view, they are probably responsible for more deaths than anything else in piking.

Within days of the Lure Society event taking place, my fears were realised. On walking around the margins of Esthwaite, I counted 43 dead pike of all sizes. I had only gone a short distance, but corpses littered the banks. It was shameful. This was one of angling's untold stories, and a buried truth. I couldn't bear it any longer and I left and have not been back since.

My dreams of a long-term first-class Northern pike water lay in tatters, thanks to the greed of the owners and the men with an obsession with using lures, no matter what the style or what the weather conditions. To me, this was the beginning of the end. There were other similar piking activities taking place in the summer months on different waters, and these also resulted in similar pike deaths. The species was being badly damaged and, ultimately, we were all to become losers.

PICTURED ABOVE

October 1990 and a superbly-conditioned 27lb 12oz fish. Another beauty from Esthwaite.

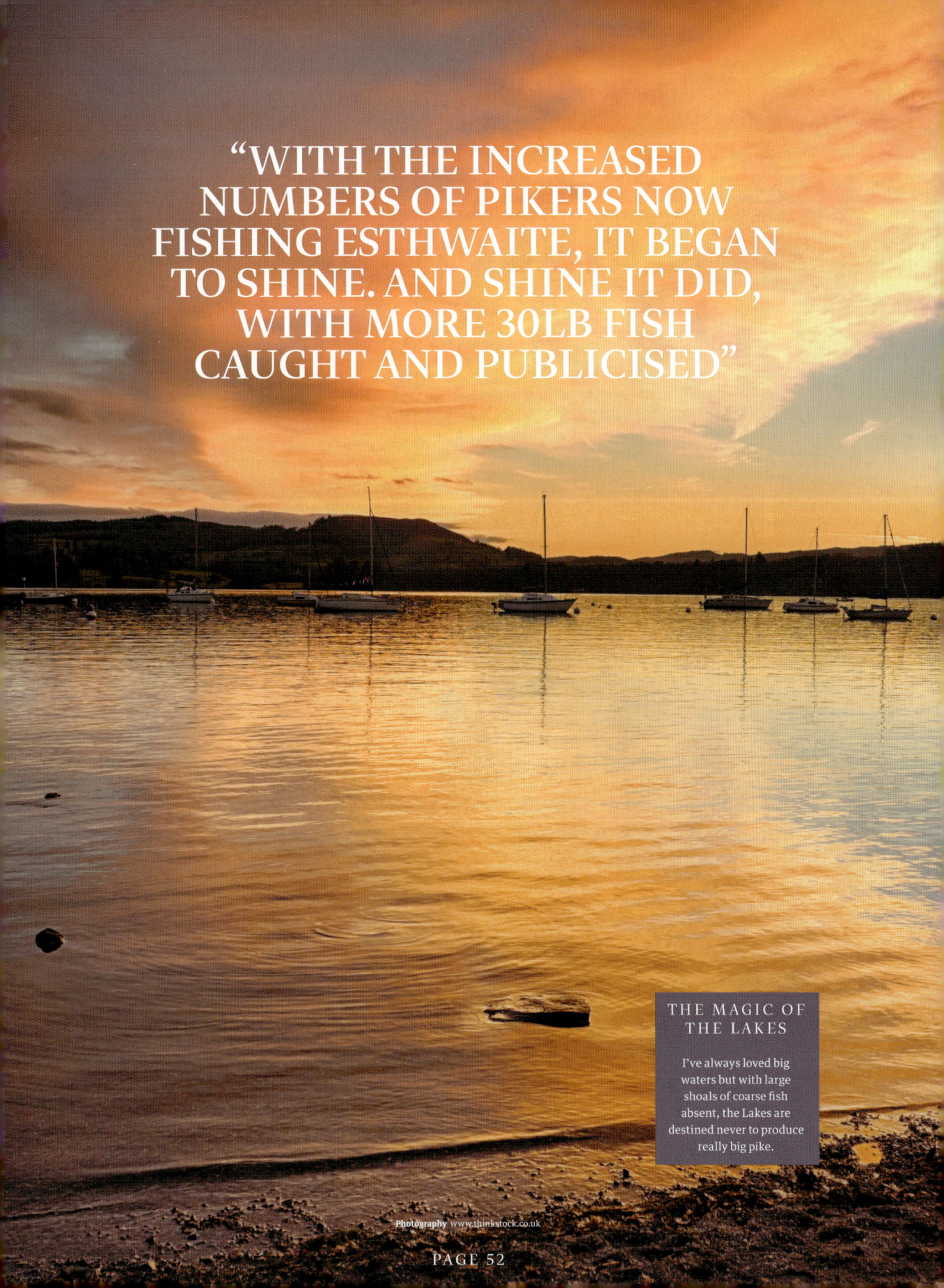

"WITH THE INCREASED NUMBERS OF PIKERS NOW FISHING ESTHWAITE, IT BEGAN TO SHINE. AND SHINE IT DID, WITH MORE 30LB FISH CAUGHT AND PUBLICISED"

THE MAGIC OF THE LAKES

I've always loved big waters but with large shoals of coarse fish absent, the Lakes are destined never to produce really big pike.

A PIKING OBSESSION

THE SCALES DON'T LIE

THE GOLDEN GLOW OF IRELAND

In my view, Ireland is probably the best pike fishing country in the World. With its vast array of different types of water, it throws up many different challenges, especially on big venues such as Lough Derg, Ree, Corrib and Mask, to name but a few. Their size makes them probably the toughest to crack, and even finding pike on these vast venues is often a task in itself.

Ireland's notorious weather - the strong winds and heavy rain that so often seem the norm - means that you often need a completely different approach to fishing than in the UK. A good-sized boat kitted

VAST, WILD AND BEAUTIFUL

The end of another day's piking in Ireland. It's the best pike fishing country in Europe, if not the World.

> " WHAT I LIKE ABOUT IRELAND IS THAT THE IRISH PEOPLE MAKE YOU FEEL VERY WELCOME AND ACTIVELY ENCOURAGE ANGLERS TO FISH THEIR WATERS"

A PIKING OBSESSION
THE SCALES DON'T LIE

out with hi-tech fish finders and GPS systems is a must, as is health and safety, and floatation suits and life jackets are essential. You're legally obliged to wear them in Ireland and only a fool goes afloat without the right kit.

Good maps of where you want to fish can be a real plus on the big waters. There are often a number of public launching spots, but sometimes they can be miles apart, and access to the waters is often via country lanes that are bereft of road signs. Getting lost in Ireland is an everyday experience - but that's part of the appeal.

The other thing I like about Ireland is that unlike in England, the Irish make you feel very welcome and actively encourage anglers to fish their waters. They'll go to great lengths to find waters that hold the species that you want to catch, explaining how best to get access, and even pre-baiting swims to help you succeed.

On one occasion I remember asking a farmer if it was okay to fish the lough from his land. When I arrived the next day, he had emptied two fields of his livestock, just in case they became a nuisance to me while I was fishing. That just wouldn't happen over here in England.

And on a recent trip to Lough Corrib, Rich and I met a local piker who enquired whether we'd been having any luck. Somewhat ruefully we had to explain that we hadn't had a take in three days, as we struggled to get to grips with Corrib on what was our first visit to the place. We asked more in hope than expectation if he could put us on

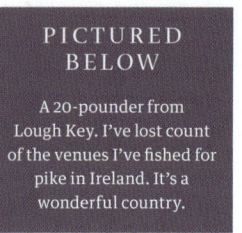

> **PICTURED BELOW**
>
> A 20-pounder from Lough Key. I've lost count of the venues I've fished for pike in Ireland. It's a wonderful country.

"THERE ARE FEWER RULES AND MORE FREEDOM TO FISH HOW AND WHEN YOU WANT"

ENJOYING THE FIGHT

Irish pike are more aggressive than their English counterparts. They hit hard and never seem to give in.

some fish, and we couldn't believe it when the next day he joined us for a guided tour of the lough close to the area where we were staying. He showed us all of the spots that produced pike recently, and over the next few days we had plenty of fish to over 20lb. There's no doubt his kindness saved us from a certain blank.

Sadly, the culture of secrecy would prevent that happening over here, with anglers too guarded (or selfish) to help out fellow fisherman. Yes, the Irish are some of the most helpful and friendly people I have ever met.

Another great thing about fishing in Ireland is that there are very few rules and lots more freedom to fish where and when you want to. Unlike the UK, it does not have a coarse fishing Close Season, with all loughs and rivers open all year round, something I believe should happen in England, too.

When I owned Burton Mere, the traditional Close Season was still in force on stillwaters as well as rivers, so I used to stock my pools with rainbow trout to get around the problem and keep the revenue coming in. I did that for years, and my coarse fish species never suffered any problems. In fact the opposite happened, and the presence of anglers on the bank deterred any feathered or furred predators, with the added bonus that my fish remained well fed between March 14 and June 16.

I have seen first-hand what happens on our rivers when they are left alone for three months. The cormorants, mink and otters have a field day. Finance also comes into my argument. The impact this ancient and outdated tradition has across the fishing

PICTURED ABOVE

Although not the intended target, ferox are a strain of trout that just have to be admired. This one came from Lough Key.

A PIKING OBSESSION
THE SCALES DON'T LIE

industry must be massive, and should be assessed and the results presented to the Environment Agency as a means of evidence. Angling numbers are dwindling fast, and fishing clubs are going to the wall, partly because they lose three months of potential earnings. This is a crazy scenario that needs to addressed urgently, in my view.

But I digress. Back to Ireland. As I said earlier, I fell in love with the place on my first visit, and I could write a number of books on my Irish adventures alone. But I'll settle with re-telling the most memorable.

Over the past eight years, Rich and I have been joined in the Emerald Isle by a group of friends and pike fanatics we call 'The Gang'. There's 'Big' Kev Shore (The Fairy), Gary Banks (The Ugly One), Paul Stephenson (Steveo) and Phil Lewis (Scouser). Between us, we've had hundreds of 20lb and 30lb fish and shared some fantastic adventures.

PICTURED ABOVE
The fishfinder is an essential tool when boatfishing in Ireland. A screen that's full of bait fish is exactly what you want to see!

I apologise in advance for some of the secrecy regarding a few of the waters, but I have done this in order to protect the pike stocks from illegal netting activities undertaken by some undesirables who would love to know where they could ply their trade.

THE GANG
From left to right: Kev Shore, Rich Lee, Phil Lewis, Paul Stephenson and yours truly. The main face missing from this picture is our old mate, Gary Banks.

A PIKING OBSESSION

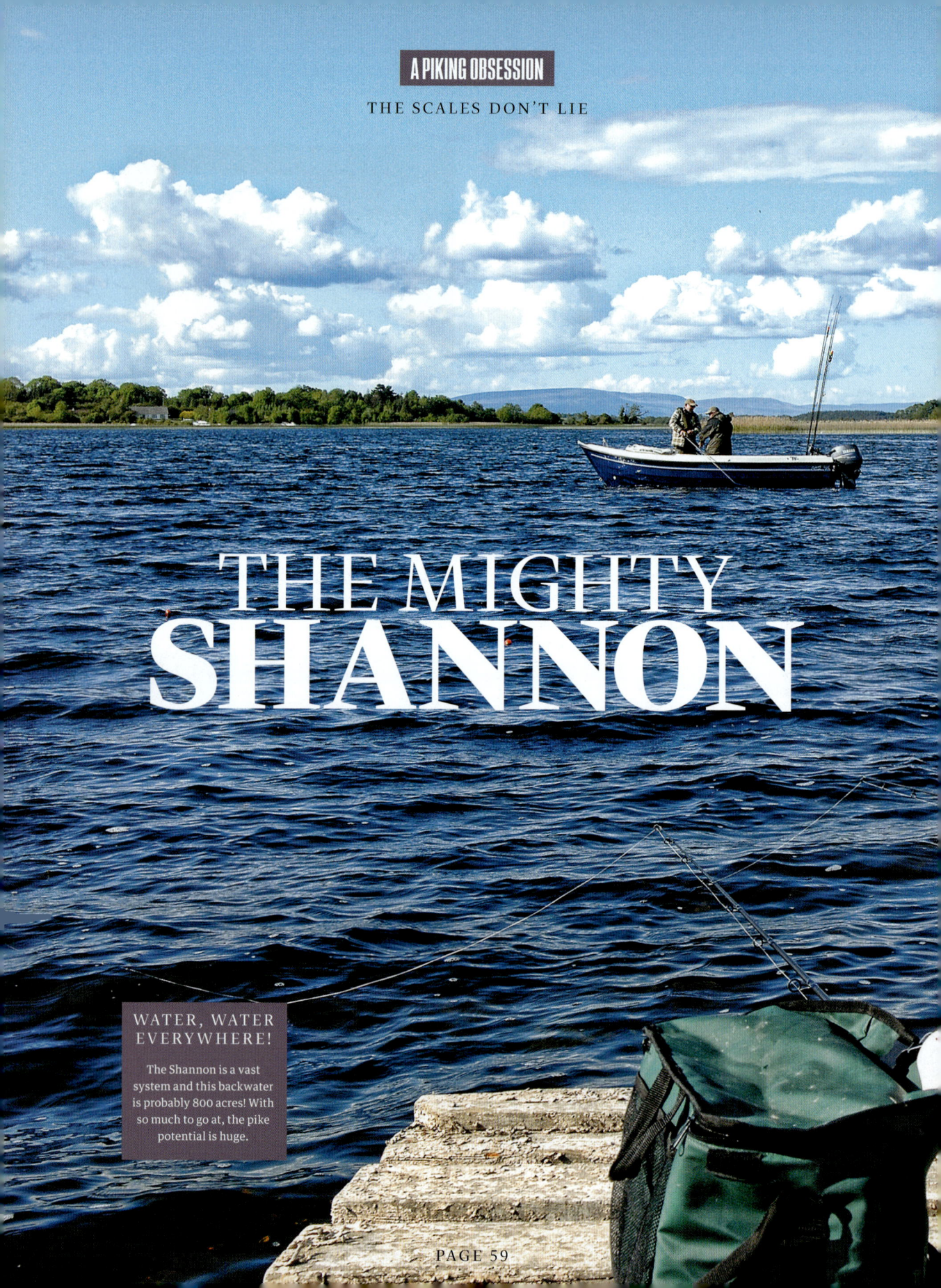

THE SCALES DON'T LIE

THE MIGHTY SHANNON

WATER, WATER EVERYWHERE!

The Shannon is a vast system and this backwater is probably 800 acres! With so much to go at, the pike potential is huge.

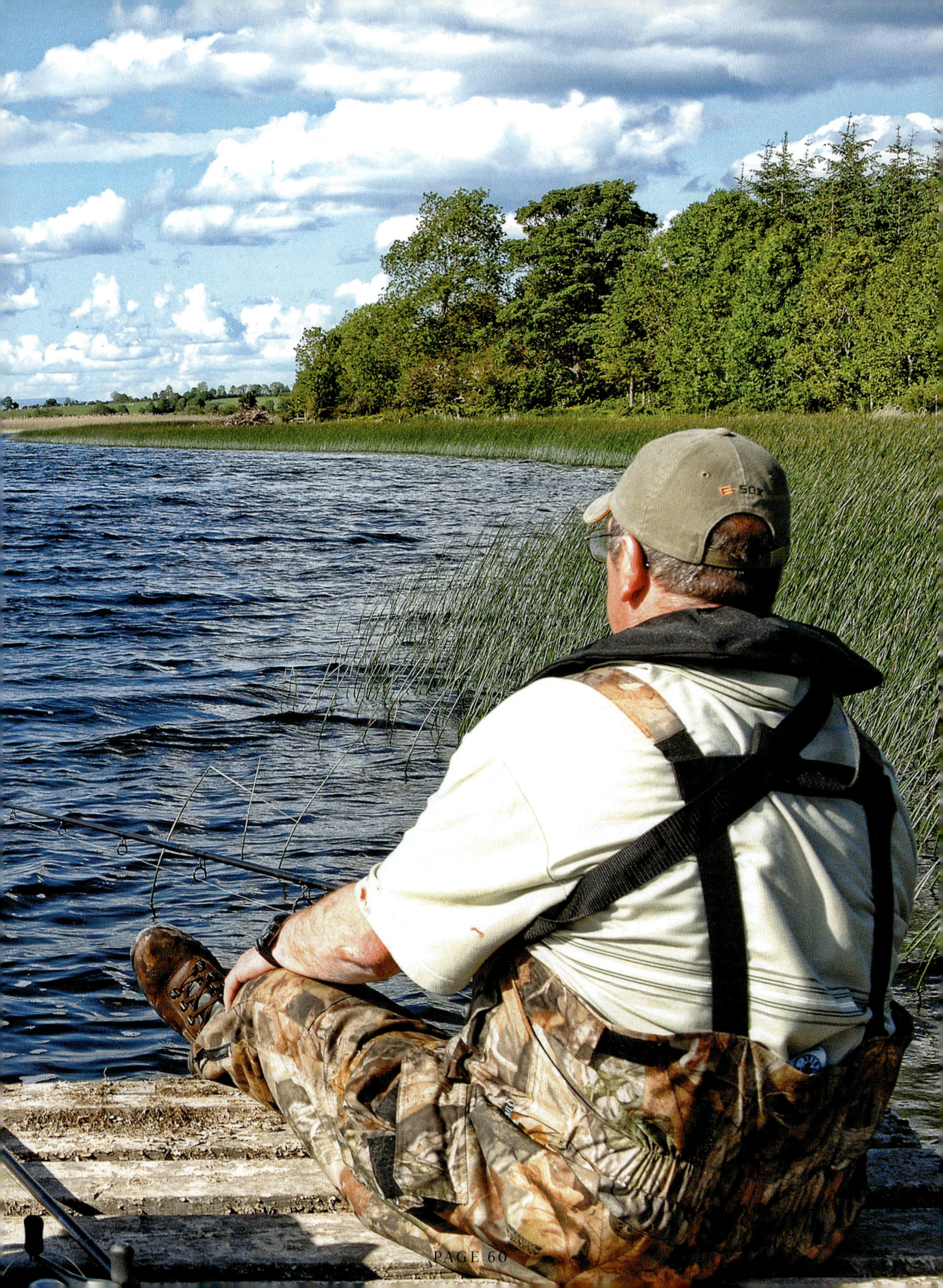
E-SOX

A PIKING OBSESSION

THE SCALES DON'T LIE

At 224 miles long, the River Shannon is Ireland's longest river, and a pike angler's Mecca. There are many loughs adjoined to it along the course, the larger ones being Lough Allen, Lough Ree and Lough Derg. These three in particular are massive sheets of water, and at times when you're fishing them, it feels as if you are out at sea, and not fishing freshwater.

There is some very limited bank fishing on the Shannon, but most of the banks are either too shallow, full of boulders or weed-fringed, so a boat is a must if you want to improve your chances of catching something.

Like all rivers, the levels often fluctuate and the water colours up, especially after heavy rainfall. It's a busy place, too, with plenty of boat traffic, mainly small cruisers that are rented to holidaymakers.

A few years ago a lot of these tourists were anglers from Europe, and on many occasions I witnessed the mass slaughter of pike. The cruisers would relentlessly troll the boat lanes with an arsenal of lures, then after catching one they would hang it over the back of boat alongside the many others that they had already caught and killed. As you can imagine, even on a river system as big as the Shannon, this sort of activity had to eventually have an effect on the pike populations, and their numbers did go down, especially on the main river.

Thankfully, after the intervention of the Irish Fisheries Board in the late 1990s, rule changes were made, one of which was to limit the size and number of fish that any individual could take home. Signs in all languages explaining the rules appeared at access points and launching spots all over Southern Ireland. This, along with the increased activity of the Fisheries Board enforcement officers, was, I believe, a major step forward in pike protection, and it's been a long while since I have seen or heard of any major fish killing taking place.

PICTURED BELOW

A twenty-pounder makes a bid for freedom. There are few finer places to fish for pike. The scenery is stunning.

PAGE 61

ON THE MOVE

Travelling from one backwater to another through the vast reedbeds that line the banks. It could be a scene from the film, The African Queen!

"AFTER A WHILE DAVE SUGGESTED THAT WE MOVE TO SOME DEEPER WATER. "IT'S SOMETHING SPECIAL," HE PROMISED....."

A PIKING OBSESSION
THE SCALES DON'T LIE

" WE CAUGHT FROM THE OFF ON SMALL DEAD ROACH, SEA BAITS, IN FACT ANYTHING WE THREW AT THEM..."

ALIVE WITH FISH!

As soon as the match anglers finished we moved in. The sport was unbelievable, with this low twenty the best of the fish.

A PIKING OBSESSION

THE SCALES DON'T LIE

> "THE BOAT WAS IN TURMOIL, AS WE RUSHED TO UNHOOK AND RETURN PIKE OF ALL SIZES, A FEW OF THEM GOING INTO HIGH TEENS"

Back in October 2006, Rich and I were invited by the Irish Tourist Board to go fishing on a number of different waters across Ireland, the idea being to assess a new guiding system that had been put in place. Portumna, a small town on the banks of the Shannon at the north end of Lough Derg, was one of the venues on the list.

On our arrival we met up with angling guide Dave Harris. He's a local lad who has spent most of his life fishing Derg, as well as the main river, and what he doesn't know about the area isn't worth knowing.

We weren't fishing long before Dave's knowledge of Derg began to bear fruit. Just out of the flow from the main river, where it entered into the lough, were a number of weedbeds, and you really couldn't have wished for a more perfect-looking pike spot. Casting our baits well away from the boat and off the bottom in 6ft of water, our floats were drifting nicely towards the weedbeds, helped by the fairly stiff breeze that had suddenly arrived.

We caught from the off, on small dead roach, sea baits, in fact almost anything that we threw at them! In just one hour we had 16 fish to 14lb, and although they weren't massive by Irish standards, we were off the mark.

After a while, Dave suggested that we move further upriver, to some deeper water marks where we might be lucky and catch a few larger fish. These areas are favoured by local match

PICTURED ABOVE

These pictures were shot for a promotional feature for the Irish Tourist Board. My face ended up all over Ireland!

PAGE 65

A PIKING OBSESSION
THE SCALES DON'T LIE

anglers, regularly producing big weights of roach and bream, so it made sense to give them a go, especially given how enthusiastic Dave was about the area.

"It's something special," he promised.

The river was about 200 metres wide, with depths to 30ft. There was a match taking place on the day, and with two hours still to go before the 'all in', we set our tackle up to do some float trolling along the far margins, well away from the match lads. Rich and I were buzzing. We were counting the minutes down, all the time thinking about Dave describing how the pike go on a feeding frenzy as they pick off their disorientated prey when they are returned to the river.

True to form, as the fish were slipped back, the water erupted with feeding pike – they were everywhere! Dave had been spot-on, and for the next 45 minutes, while the match weigh-in was being done, we never stopped catching! The boat was in utter turmoil, as we rushed to unhook and return pike of all sizes, a few of them going into the high teens.

Then, all of a sudden, calm returned. The pike had finished feeding and it was, or so we thought, all over. But my float disappeared one more time and soon a beautifully conditioned low 20-pounder graced my landing net. We were completely knackered, but it was a fabulous 45 minutes, and something that Rich and I will never forget.

> **PICTURED ABOVE**
>
> I told you they fight like hell in Ireland! The rod takes the strain as a powerful fish refuses to give in.

A PIKING OBSESSION

THE SCALES DON'T LIE

LIFE & NEAR DEATH ON LOUGH REE

HEADING BACK HOME

Rich steers the boat home after a day on Lough Ree. It's a big and dangerous water that can make you feel very vulnerable at times.

A PIKING OBSESSION
THE SCALES DON'T LIE

Lough Ree had been on our 'radar' for some time. It is one of the larger loughs that are connected to the River Shannon, and over the years we'd heard of many large pike being caught from its waters. Unsurprisingly, The Gang was eager to give it a try.

On a number of trips to Ree, our digs were self-catering units on a golfing complex, which is based at the southern end of the lough. At the time we thought it was the ideal location to explore this massive water. However, what we didn't appreciate was that the water we could see in front of the golf club was, in fact, more like a massive bay that was joined to Ree by a 100-metre-wide channel.

We found out later that it was a lough in its own right, called Killinure. It absolutely screamed pike. There were plenty of weedbeds and drop-offs, and food fish were always showing on the echo-sounder. But we soon learned that waters that look good don't always live up to expectations, and after many days of trying to find some decent-sized fish in Killinure, we decided that life was too short. Ree had to be a better option.

Rich and I will never forget our first trip onto the main lough. It was a wake-up call that reminded us of the danger we face every time we fish large waters. The weather was fine when we left the digs, although the forecast for later in the day warned of gale-force winds. The other members of The Gang wisely decided that they wouldn't venture far, to avoid the risk of getting caught out.

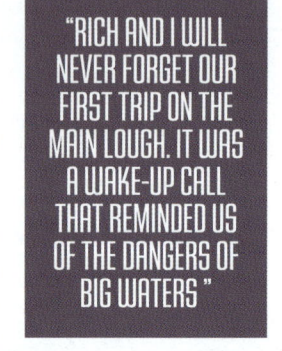

> "RICH AND I WILL NEVER FORGET OUR FIRST TRIP ON THE MAIN LOUGH. IT WAS A WAKE-UP CALL THAT REMINDED US OF THE DANGERS OF BIG WATERS"

TAKING TO THE AIR
A mid-double breaks the surface in a bid to shake the hooks. Ree is a huge water with vast fishless areas.

On reflection, Rich and I were a pair of plonkers. We took a risk, heading out into the main lough, naively believing that we had time to turn around if the weather became inclement.

We made our way to a small group of islands on the west side of Ree, a trip that took around 45 minutes. It was an area that had been marked on our map by a local piker who had been catching fish from there for many years.

For a couple of hours we trolled our deadbaits around the islands with no success, and it was not until we moved out approximately 200 metres into deeper water that we started to catch a few small pike. By now there was a light wind blowing, and we opted to use the drogue instead of the engine to drift across the better areas.

> **PICTURED ABOVE**
>
> A low twenty from Lough Ree. We've enjoyed some great days on the water but when the weather turns, it can be cruel.

For the next couple of hours we enjoyed plenty of action, landing a few doubles and a low 'twenty' each. But in all the excitement, we hadn't noticed just how much the wind had increased outside the protection of the islands.

We quickly agreed it was time to make a run for it before it got any worse.

As we made our way back across the large expanse of open water, it soon became obvious we had left it too late. The wind was now blowing seriously hard and we were stuck in the middle of no man's land. The waves were in the 7ft to 8ft feet range and to make matters worse, it was simply too dangerous to turn the boat around or sideways - with the height of the waves we would have almost certainly been swamped. I remember looking skyward and hoping ➤

that Him up there was watching over us because we were in serious need of his help.

All we could do was keep the bow of the boat pointing into the coming swell, allow the engine to tick over and creep forward very, very slowly. If we'd have gone too fast, the bow would have ridden far too high on a wave and we'd have come crashing down into the next one. This would have seriously damaged the boat, not to mention us, so slow and steady was the best we could achieve. At times it was difficult to keep seated when the boat was tossing and turning so much.

After about an hour of this hell, we came into slightly calmer water, where we could increase our speed towards safety. We had made it. I can't describe the relief I felt as we saw the sanctuary of the golf club. Him upstairs had indeed kept us safe and we'd made it. The stiff drink we enjoyed later that night tasted sweeter than ever.

That same year Rich and I were back at the place after receiving an invite from the Irish Tourist Board to join a group of pike angling journalists who'd come from all over Europe. The intention was to hold a yearly pike fishing festival on Lough Ree, and we were assembled as part of a 'test run' to assess any potential logistical problems in organising such a competition.

We had a great time. It was good to meet fellow journalists, and the three-day event was a massive success, with many fish to over 20lb. I understand that it's now a very successful annual event, and in 2013, 180 anglers took part, fishing for a prize fund of 17,000 Euros.

On our next few trips with The Gang, we changed our digs to a more suitable location - somewhere that gave us quicker (and safer) journeys to the main lough and our intended fishing areas. On most occasions when the weather was good, the fishing matched it, and over the coming months we all caught plenty of good-sized pike, a dozen of which topped 20lb.

Our new digs came with an added advantage beyond location - it had its own boat moorings. The only really drawback being that when it was windy, it was very difficult to get back through the entrance, to the safety of the moorings. The gap was very narrow, and either side made of concrete, meaning that if we got our approach wrong, the boat could be badly damaged.

One day Rich and I had a real nightmare attempting to negotiate it. We tried numerous times to approach the entrance at the right speed, but there was a 3ft swell blowing across the front of it and the danger was that the wind could force the boat against the walls. To make matters worse, the other members of The Gang were standing in the windows of our digs taking the mick and laughing their heads off at our continued attempts to get our approach right.

> "WE SMASHED INTO THE WALL AND A PIECE OF FIBRELASS THAT SHOULD HAVE BEEN ATTACHED TO THE FRONT OF THE BOAT FLEW OVER MY SHOULDER"

It was at this point that I asked Rich to sit at the front of the boat and put his legs out directly ahead of him. My idea was that he could cushion any contact with the concrete walls, while I opened the throttle and tried to push through the entrance at speed. I planned to shove the engine into reverse once we were through, to slow us down.

It seemed like a great plan... or so I thought. From my end, everything went well - we were all but through and the engine was soon in reverse. But I had not allowed for Rich's meagre attempt to cushion any impact with the concrete wall with his legs. They folded like jelly! We then smashed into the wall and a piece of fibreglass that should have been

PART OF THE PIKE ARSENAL

A selection of small lures. As I've mentioned, I'm not a huge fan of lures and limit my selection to nothing bigger than six inches.

attached to the front of the boat, flew over my shoulder and into the lough.

For the next ten minutes Rich and I had words, arguing over who was to blame. I accused him of being too weak, while he reckoned I'd just gone too fast. All of this, of course, was played out in front of The Gang, who were, by this time, rolling around with laughter.

But a bad day was about to get worse. During the week, Ugly and The Big Fairy had been feeding sausages to the dirtiest three-legged dog you have ever seen. It was a manky stray, and the thing had become a bloody nuisance. As Rich and I entered the digs, I commented that there was no sign of the mutt. Blank looks stared back at me.

After removing my wet clothing and placing it on the kitchen radiator to dry, I had a cup of coffee and a well-earned cigar before making my way to my room. I walked in, shut my door and in complete darkness fumbled for my bedside light. As I sat down on the bed there was such an almighty squeal - I'd sat on the bloody dog! I swore revenge as The Gang fell about with laughter.

We had a few more trips to Lough Ree over the coming months, but the largest fish caught was by The Big Fairy at 24lb 8oz. I have no doubt that there are bigger fish to be taken from Ree, but life can be too short at times, and we were ready to continue our search for another water.

A PIKING OBSESSION
THE SCALES DON'T LIE

LONG AND LEAN

The calm before the storm. This low twenty came shortly before the weather turned. When it did, it made it a dangerous place to be.

The DANGERS OF LOUGH DERG

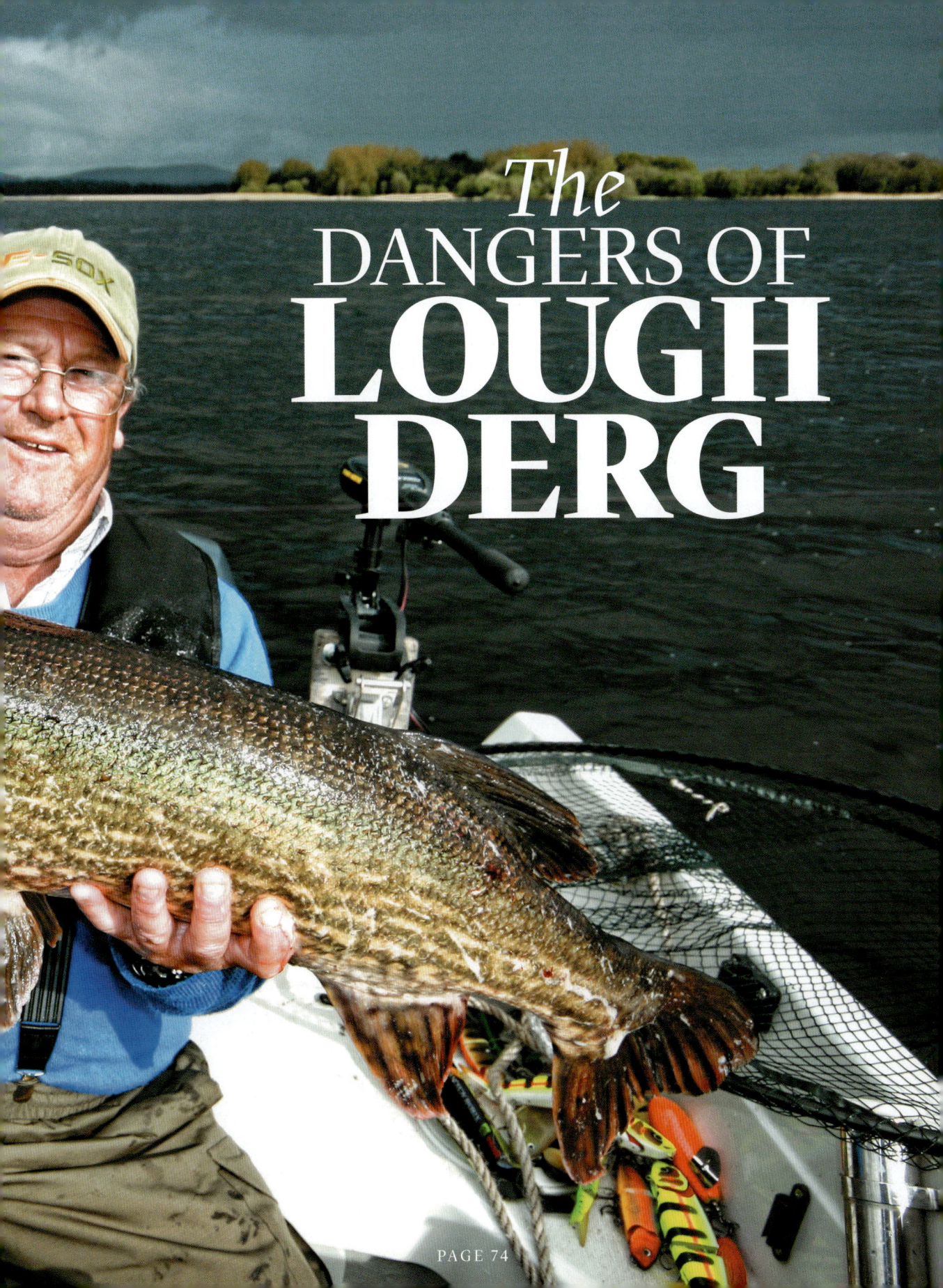

PAGE 74

HIT AND HOLD!

That solid feeling when you hit a pike take still gives me the same pleasure as it's always done. At that point you don't know if the fish is 5lb or 25lb.

A PIKING OBSESSION

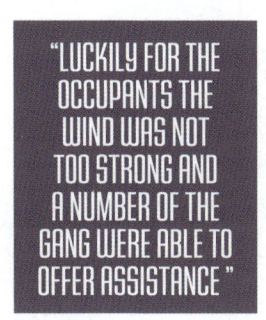

THE SCALES DON'T LIE

Derg is one of Ireland's most dangerous loughs, and on a windy day, you venture away from the main boating lanes at your peril. The many bays around the lough - which is a massive 30 miles long - scream pike, but all too often we are disappointed when we find that they are shallow and boulder-strewn, and not as perfect as we were hoping for.

We know one of the large bays well, and it's where The Gang have caught plenty of fish, but it was also the scene of a near disaster. A small cabin cruiser diverted away from the main boating lane and headed in the direction of the bay. Within moments it hit the rocks and just lay there on the surface of the water. It didn't take long for it to list to one side, filling up fast as it did so.

Luckily for the occupants, the wind was not too strong at the time and a number of The Gang were fishing close, and able to offer assistance. Steveo and Phil were soon on the scene, but they couldn't take the chance of getting any closer than 40 metres, because they, too, would have run aground.

Steveo made a quick 999 call to the UK authorities, who in turn informed the Irish emergency rescue services. But in the meantime the two occupants of the boat were sitting very precariously on the side of their upturned vessel.

> "LUCKILY FOR THE OCCUPANTS THE WIND WAS NOT TOO STRONG AND A NUMBER OF THE GANG WERE ABLE TO OFFER ASSISTANCE"

GOLDEN GLOW

I think it's the size of the loughs in Ireland that make them so attractive. Some of the fish have probably never seen a hook before.

A PIKING OBSESSION
THE SCALES DON'T LIE

A short while later a small 'rib' sped across the surface of the lough in our direction. It was the ideal boat to go in close to rescue the now wet and cold occupants, but I dread to think what the outcome would have been if the wind had been stronger or we had not been around to ring for help.

When a strong wind is blowing down or up the lough, it can be genuinely scary. The waves can reach a height of 6ft to 7ft at times, and that might not seem too bad to hardened seafarers in their off-shore boats, but to us pikers in our smaller vessels, it can frighten the hell out of us!

However when the conditions are right, the fishing on Derg can be awesome. All of The Gang have caught many 'twenties' from different areas of the lough: Scouser Phil had one at 27lb 12oz, and The Big Fairy, (aka Kev Shore) took a fish of 26lb 8oz. These two are the largest that The Gang has managed, although there are 30lb-plus pike taken every year from the place.

So even with the dangerous wind and the perilous rocks, it's a venue I will continue my search for bigger pike.

> **PICTURED ABOVE**
> Rich with a truly magnificent 14lb 10oz ferox trout. He was as chuffed with this as he would have been with a 30lb pike!

SIMPLY MAGIC

I've been fortunate enough to catch more twenties from Ireland than I can remember. But every single one is a pleasure.

"THE WAVES CAN REACH 6FT OR 7FT AT TIMES AND TO PIKERS IN SMALL VESSELS, IT CAN FRIGHTEN THE HELL OUT OF US!"

ONE MORE CAST

The sun begins to set on another day's Irish piking. Lough Ramor is a huge venue but you need to find the fish to be successful.

A PIKING OBSESSION

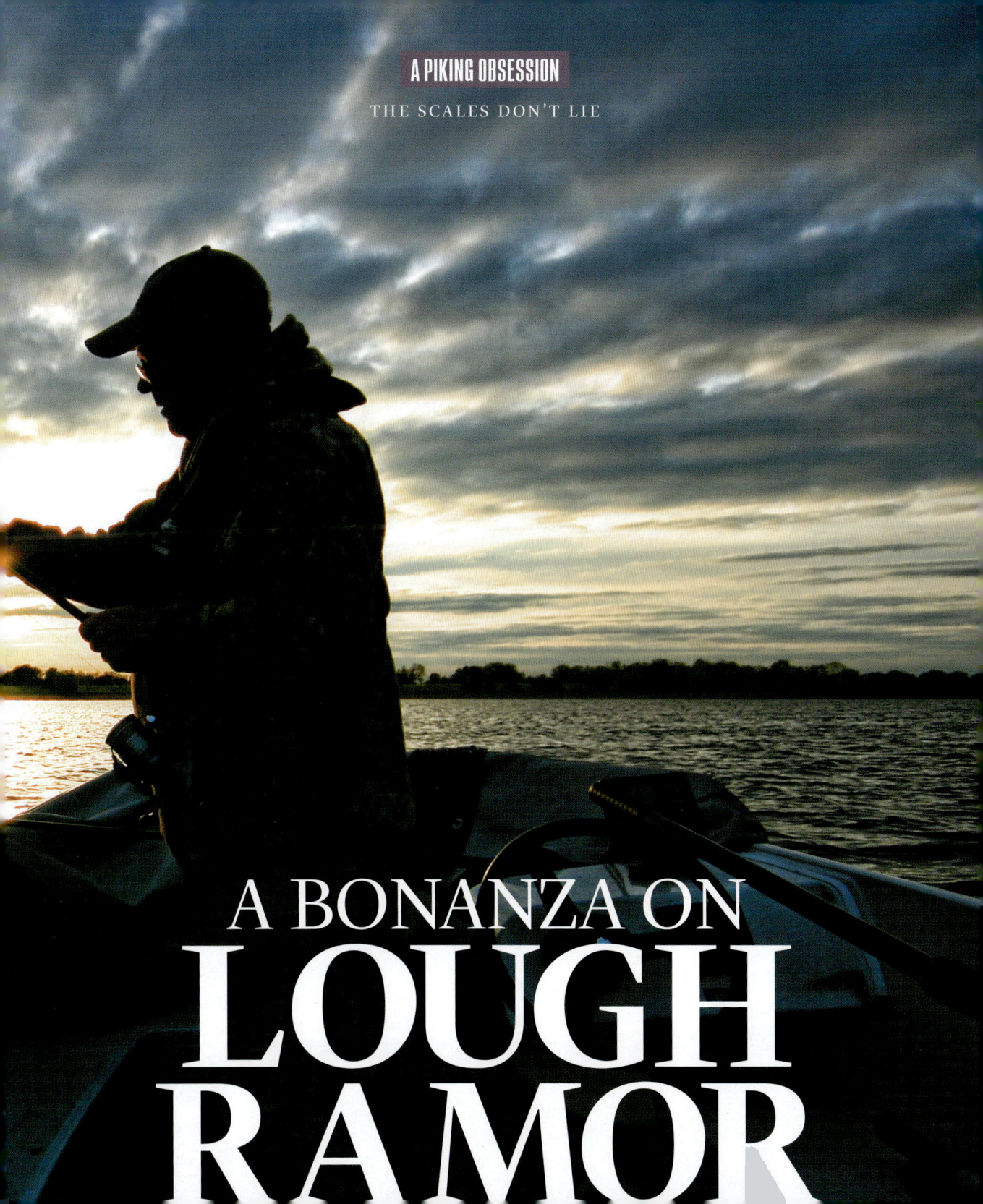

THE SCALES DON'T LIE

A BONANZA ON
LOUGH
RAMOR

TRYING TO BE DIFFERENT

This rig, known as the Christmas Tree, proved to be brilliant. You put a small fish on each treble and troll. It's highly visible in the water.

A PIKING OBSESSION

THE SCALES DON'T LIE

When Rich and I were assessing would-be fishing guides for the Irish Tourist Board in 2006, we had an invite to fish with two of them on Lough Ramor, in County Cavan. We didn't know it at the time, but the pike fishing on Ramor was so good it had been kept a closely guarded secret for a number of years by the local anglers and even the guides.

It wasn't until the last day of that particular trip that we met the two lads in the car park of the Lakeside Hotel, near Virginia. After a few minutes chatting and listening to their exploits, we couldn't wait to get afloat. Soon enough we were, I was with one guide and Rich the other… the competition to catch the most pike was on.

The guides' preferred method of fishing was to troll big lures out of the back of the boat, covering the many features that they had found over the years. We soon learnt they knew the place like the back of their hand, which was a good thing because on a number of occasions I spotted rocks lying just under the surface of the water. Without their knowledge and guidance, Rich and I would certainly have been dicing with death.

For me the day was a complete disaster - one lost fish and that was it. Rich, on the other hand, battered them, taking a dozen pike to low 'twenties'. I remember, as we supped a few pints later that night, saying that he must have had the better guide!

It wasn't long before we were booked into the Lakeside Hotel for a week, only this time we were joined by Steveo, Scouser and The Big Fairy. We started each day full of expectation, but what a disappointment the week turned

> **PICTURED BELOW**
> A quality mid-double from Ramor. For a couple of years The Gang spent a lot of time targeting the pike on what can be a patchy water.

PAGE 82

"THE GIGANTIC CONCENTRATION OF SHOAL FISH MUST HAVE ATTRACTED VIRTUALLY EVERY PIKE IN THE LOUGH, ALL KEEN TO GORGE ON THIS NATURAL BOUNTY"

A PIKING OBSESSION
THE SCALES DON'T LIE

WHAT IT'S ALL ABOUT
Battling a good fish on a big Irish lough is my idea of angling heaven. I try and savour every moment.

A PIKING OBSESSION
THE SCALES DON'T LIE

> "A COUPLE OF WEEKS AFTER SPAWNING WAS OVER, I WAS BACK ON THE LOUGH, THIS TIME ALONE, FOR A SHORT THREE-DAY SESSION"

out to be, with just a handful of fish to 17lb. Our timing had been awful. The fish were in full spawning mode and completely uninterested in feeding.

But what we saw gave us grounds for encouragement. We had observed numerous 20lb-plus pike at very close quarters, seemingly oblivious to our presence, which at times was near enough to pick them up, and witnessing this convinced us that Ramor deserved more time and effort.

A couple of weeks after the spawning was over, I was back on the lough, this time alone, for a short three-day session. The weather was perfect, with only light winds forecast for the duration of my stay.

The first day out was disappointing. While float trolling with herring over all the areas from which we had previously caught some fish, I didn't manage a single run. I just couldn't work it out, and was all but resigned to returning to the hotel with my tail between my legs.

With just an hour of daylight left, I was tired of trolling, so I put the anchors down in 7ft of water and cast my baits either side of the boat. Would you believe it, ten minutes later my float sank out of sight and I was soon into a fish of about 17lb. However, what was really interesting was that the commotion caused by playing that fish had spooked a number of other pike that were clearly in the vicinity. With a smile back

PICTURED ABOVE

Pike fishing can be a waiting game but there were spells on Ramor where the sport was absolutely exceptional.

PAGE 85

on my face, I felt sure I'd located the right area, and the next day was suddenly looking good.

Come first light I was back on the lough and heading in the direction of where I'd caught the previous evening's 17-pounder. By now there was a light wind blowing down the lough, in contrast to the flat-calm nature of 24 hours earlier.

The fish that I had spotted the day before were in relatively shallow water, so to avoid spooking them, I decided to give the area a wide birth and then, with the help of the wind, slowly drift the boat over to where I had seen them. Using the full length of the vessel, my two rods were set to fish down to 3ft deep and were baited with whole herring.

> **PICTURED ABOVE**
>
> Boat fishing on Ramor. It's a huge venue but the pike stocks are concentrated in small pockets.

As soon as I reached my target spot, one of my floats slipped away. Bingo! I was in the process of slipping the net under a fish close to 20lb when I got a take on the other rod. It wasn't long before another large pike joined the one already in the landing net.

For a few moments it was total chaos in the boat, but having experienced double hook-ups before, I was soon organised and the fish were safely unhooked, weighed and returned to the water. At 19lb 5oz and 22lb, they were a great start to the day.

I enjoyed another two double hook-ups on what turned out to be a brilliant day's fishing. The final tally was 22, 18 of which were doubles, together with one 'twenty' and three jacks.

PAGE 86

> " AS SOON AS WE ARRIVED WE COULD SEE FISH ROLLING ON THE SURFACE EVERYWHERE WE LOOKED..."

What a day to remember! But what I didn't know at the time was that there was to be an even better one to come…

In October of that same year, The Gang and I were back on the water. The only person missing was Gary (or Ugly), who said he couldn't make it because he had to work for a living.

The weather forecast for the first part of the week was good, but typically of Ireland, gales were then due to arrive later on, to be joined by torrential rain. We would have to 'make hay' over the first four days.

The three boats were out on the lough at first light and, as normal, The Big Fairy, with his super-sized engine and boat, was speeding way out in front, followed by Steveo and Scouser, with Rich and I bringing up the rear. Our 14ft Orkney - now nicknamed 'The Slug Boat' - together with 15-horse Yamaha had no chance of catching them and their 30-horse engines. Posers!

We headed for an area of the lough with depths down to 40ft in places. With many underwater features and having provided limited success in the past, it was as good a place to start as any. The water was flat calm - a rare occurrence on a lough of 2,000-acres - making it perfect for float trolling on the electric engine. With the water gin clear, the pike could spot and attack our moving deadbaits with ease. We could not have picked a better place to begin.

PICTURED ABOVE

A beautifully-marked 25lb 8oz Ramor fish. Pike don't come much better looking.

PAGE 87

A PIKING OBSESSION

THE SCALES DON'T LIE

As soon as we arrived we could see fish rolling on the surface; they were everywhere we looked. The fish-finders soon told us why there were so many predators about, as there was a large grey line showing on the screen, indicating that 6ft below the surface were masses of small fish.

This was soon confirmed when we unhooked the first pike of the day, landed by Rich. Small roach spewed out of its mouth as we removed the hooks, and it was obvious the pike had been gorging themselves on the masses of small fish in attendance. And when I say 'masses', I mean masses. I had never seen so many. After trolling for a few hours in different directions we estimated the size of the shoal to be around half a square mile, most of them made up of fry, but with the odd bigger fish among them.

This gigantic concentration must have attracted virtually every pike in the lough, all keen to gorge on this natural bounty. We, in turn, were able to enjoy the time of our lives, and we rarely trolled more than 100 metres before our floats disappeared beneath the surface.

All three boats caught many pike of all sizes, mainly to trolled deadbaits, and at the time it was the best four days' piking any of us had ever had. While having a pint on the fourth night, The Gang agreed we'd caught between us somewhere around 3,000lb of fish, including nine 'twenties' to 25lb 8oz, the latter of which luckily fell to my rod.

Once again all good things come to an end. Word got out and more and more pike anglers started to appear on the lough. The inevitable decline soon followed, and after many good pike fishing trips to Ramor, it was now time for us to move on. It's a venue of which all of us still have fond memories, and we will certainly return for an occasional trip in the future.

PICTURED BELOW

A good fish lies beaten in the net, while Rich watches on as a mid-double takes to the air. Ramor has provided us with some superb sport.

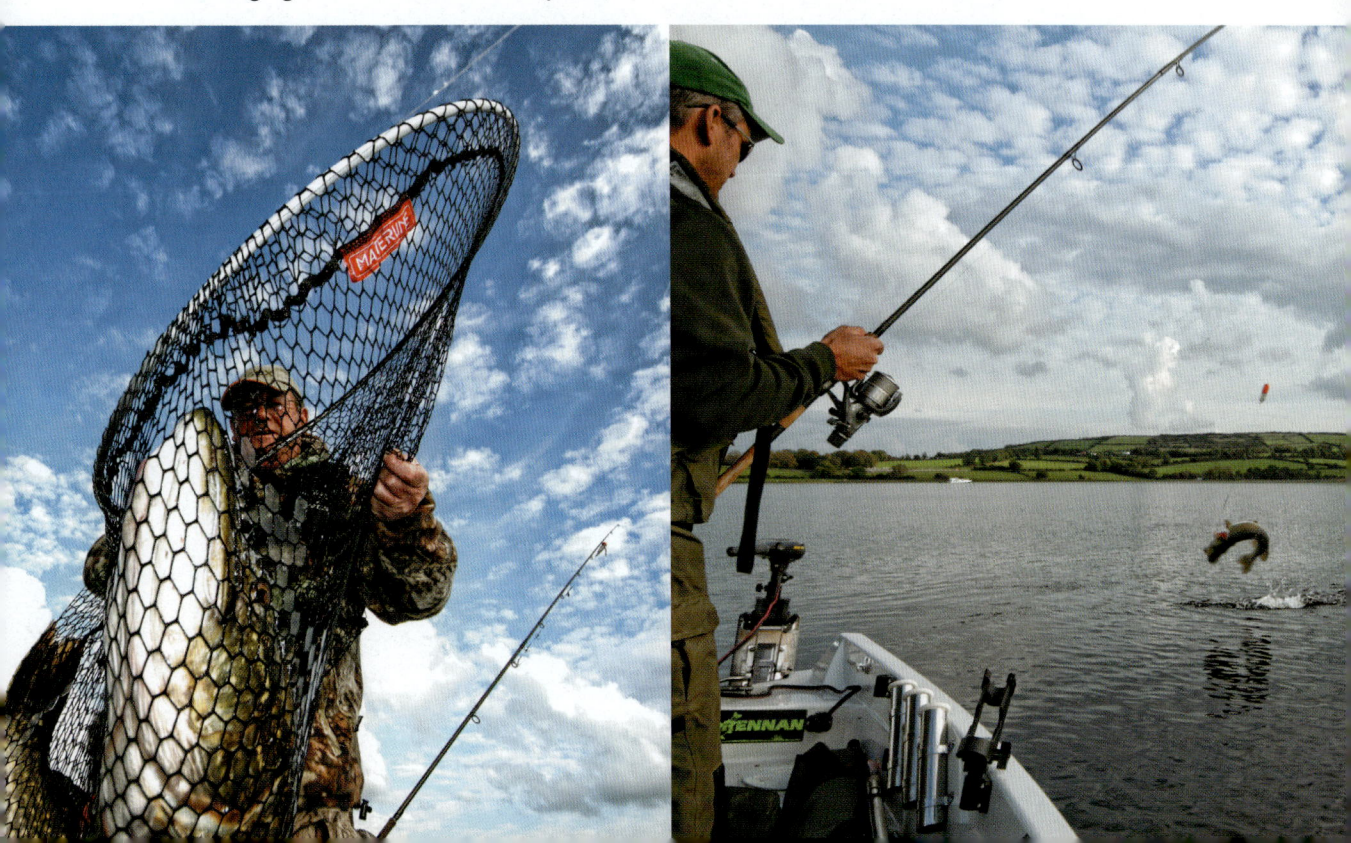

WHAT A FIGHT!

A trip to the Upper Shannon in 2009 provided a brilliant week's fishing... and plenty of banter among the boys!

A PIKING OBSESSION

THE SCALES DON'T LIE

FUN & GAMES ON THE UPPER SHANNON

In October 2009 The Gang decided we would have a return trip to the Upper Shannon, specifically to an area that has many large and small loughs adjoining the main river. It was a region we knew reasonably well, and where we'd all had reasonable success, catching plenty of doubles and a few 20lb-plus fish, too.

Unlike on the large open loughs, there are plenty of places where you can shelter from the worst of the weather, so when there's a big blow on, you can always find somewhere to fish. The accommodation we use is also perfect: two self-catering houses sit on the edge of the river, and on this particular occasion The Big Fairy, Ugly and Scouser were in one, Steveo, Rich and I were in the other. The digs also come with the massive advantage of a well-secured boat marina that includes CCTV.

You cannot beat this all-too-rare convenience. With it goes the daily rigmarole of attaching the boat to the car, parking it safely and then unloading the kit. Instead, you get up in the morning, make a flask, pack your lunch,

A PIKING OBSESSION
THE SCALES DON'T LIE

pick up fresh bait and then get fishing. Perfect!

The amount of water to fish in this area is massive. Sometimes we travel as far as eight miles in the boats to some of the far-flung reaches of the loughs. With 99 per cent of the banksides being weed-fringed, you have no choice but to go afloat and in the winter months you're lucky to see another angler or boat. It really is another of Ireland's pike Meccas.

The only trouble with these Gang trips is being in the company of Ugly and The Big Fairy (I love them really!). Sometimes, and especially when they are together, they can be a pain in the arse – the mickey-taking is relentless, and the rest of us have to be on our guard not to provide them with any ammunition.

One very wet day we were all fishing on the main river when Ugly and The Big Fairy decided they'd had enough of the rain. When they said they were heading back to the digs, we gave them plenty of stick. Real men, we let them know, would carry on fishing. Half an hour later we spotted Steveo and Scouser speeding down the lough in our direction. Rich and I thought they were having an early day, too, but it was clear they wanted to speak to us urgently.

"I think I've dropped a right bollock," said Steveo.

When I asked why, he quickly explained that he'd given Ugly the key to our digs. Big error. The wind-up merchants would have a field day.

"You bloody plonker," I spluttered, before Rich and I gathered our kit together in double quick time before heading back to the accommodation.

As Rich, Steveo and I arrived at the front door, it reminded me of a Police swat team entering a building. We started to check all the ground floor rooms first. All clear. We then moved upstairs to do a sweep of the bedrooms and toilet. All clear. It was the same in Rich's room, then Steveo's. Only mine left.

As I tried to open the door, it thudded against something very solid – the bastards had somehow managed to move my wardrobe to the back of the door.

As I turned round, the pair of them were laughing their heads off.

But even I cracked a smile when they told me they were going to trash Rich's room, but it was so untidy it wouldn't have looked any different!

The fishing over the first couple of days of that trip was a bit slow, which is not unusual. With such a lot of water to cover, it does often take time to access the likely areas to catch pike. The best way that we find to assess a water is to float-troll our baits out the back of the boat and cover those fancied spots. With the help of the electric motor, you can do this nice and slowly, and with the aid of our fish-finder we are able to spot any concentrations of silver fish.

By the third day, The Gang had covered a lot of water and a picture was beginning to form. What fish we had caught had, in the main, come from the deeper areas, in particular where there were pockets of roach and bream. Over a distance of eight miles, crossing the water from bank to bank, we had located four spots where the depths dropped down to 40ft and more. The Gang decided these were the areas most likely to hold a few pike and were worth some effort over

> **PICTURED BELOW**
> Pike fishing can be a serious business but I've always tried to have a laugh along the way. Fishing's supposed to be fun, after all.

BOYS WILL BE BOYS..

Gary and Big Kev do a number on Rich! But the buggers had the last laugh when they revealed what they'd done to my toothbrush!

the coming days.

Almost from the off the concentrated effort was starting to pay off. Pike were beginning to fall to all three boats, and when one of the areas went quiet, we moved to another. And so on. When we had finished fishing the fourth of the chosen spots, we would return to the first and catch more pike.

The concentration or silver fish was unbelievable. There was so many of them that we were able to watch them swimming around the boats. Some were bream that were maybe up to 8lb, and swimming with them were thousands of skimmers and roach.

By the end of the week we had collectively caught an estimated 2,500lb of pike, many of which were well into double figures. The masses of food fish must have attracted predators from miles around, and the only disappointing part of the week was that only one low 'twenty' had fallen, taken by Ugly.

It was four days later, as we were on the ferry back home, that we were discussing the events of our adventure, and analysing, as always, the highs and lows. After ten minutes of listening to Ugly harp on about being the only one to catch a 'twenty', I decided to change the conversation and ask why he and The Big Fairy had gone so easy on our piss-taking and why, given the golden opportunity of having the house key, they had been relatively lenient. I should have smelt a rat when the two of them suddenly broke out in fits of laughter.

"Come on then," I said. "What's so funny?"

"How often do you brush your teeth, Tel?," asked Ugly, in between fits of giggles.

"Twice every day. Why?" I replied, a worried feeling growing in the pit of my stomach.

Gary, aka Ugly, reached into his pocket, took out his phone and within a few seconds presented me with a picture on the screen. I couldn't believe it. There was my toothbrush planted firmly between the cheeks of his bare arse. Bastards!

A PIKING OBSESSION
THE SCALES DON'T LIE

'WHAT'S IT WEIGH?'
I take the strain and wait for the verdict.... The Secret Water provided our best week for big fish ever.

SUCCESS
ON THE SECRET WATER

A PIKING OBSESSION

THE SCALES DON'T LIE

I must apologise straight away for not naming the venue. Just referring to it as 'The Secret Water' is not a completely selfish act, as there are many good reasons why I cannot divulge its name and location. The water is highly thought of by local anglers, a lot of whom, over the years, have become friends of mine, and I would like to respect their wishes and protect it from over-fishing.

There is another very good reason for my secrecy, and that is the extremes that some idiots will go to in order to protect their fishing can sometimes go well over the top. This I'll explain in more detail later in the chapter.

My first visit to the The Secret Water was back in the mid-'90s. I had received an invitation from Cheshire big-fish specialist Graham Marsden to join him and a few others to sample the pike fishing that they'd been enjoying on the lough for the past two winters.

My first view of the place gave me goosebumps. It looked like the perfect pike water; reed-fringed, very shallow, in the middle of nowhere and, crucially, free from serious angling pressure. The only notable potential issue was the prolific weed - it was so bad in places there was no point in fishing until January or February, when most of it had died back.

Over the next couple of years we managed to fish there a couple of times each winter, but with mixed results on each visit. If conditions were kind to us, the fishing seemed to be better, and we managed occasional 'twenties'. The trouble is, the weather in this part of ➤

> **PICTURED BELOW**
> Readying the boat for a day's fishing. The anticipation that greets each day keeps me going, no matter what the weather.

SECRET LAKE SUCCESS

Rich waits for a bite, while (top left) I cradle a 22lb 14oz fish (top right). Below: This 28lb 8oz monster is my best Irish pike.

A PIKING OBSESSION
THE SCALES DON'T LIE

"IT WAS FANTASTIC FISHING THAT PRODUCED 14 TWENTIES AND WE LOST COUNT OF THE DOUBLES, MANY OF THEM HIGH TEENS"

ALL SMILES

Rich with a low twenty. He caught it just before a big storm sent us reeling for cover.

A PIKING OBSESSION
THE SCALES DON'T LIE

> "IN NOVEMBER 2012 THE GANG AND I RETURNED WITHOUT RICH FOR WHAT PROVED TO BE A VERY SPECIAL WEEK..."

Ireland is renowned for being bad in the winter, its proximity to the Atlantic Ocean ensuring that rain, winds and often snow blows in from the coast in January and February in particular.

On one of the early visits lasting a week, we found conditions to be perfect, apart from the temperatures dropping to -7 Centigrade each night! On our first day we arrived at the water early in the morning and you would have thought we were in Alaska, not Ireland - there was not a cloud in the sky and it was freezing cold. The water was glass calm and a thin layer of ice covered the entire lough.

"Great," said Graham, "what are we supposed to do now?"

"Have a cup of tea and piker's bacon butty," was my reply.

PICTURED ABOVE

Steveo sits in one of the boats before a day on the water. The venue provided us with brilliant fishing over a period of years.

I had experienced similar conditions before on large waters and I knew that as the day progressed, some wind was bound to make an appearance and when it did, with the help of the sun, the temperatures would soon rise, causing the ice to melt. But before all that we could help nature by using our boat as an ice-breaker. This would allow the wind to remove the ice a lot quicker. A small, one-man boat is no good for fishing from, but it's a great tool when bank fishing for transporting baits beyond casting range, and it was also the ideal tool for breaking the ice and allowing the wind to blow it away.

As we supped our tea, we agreed on a small wager: each man threw in a tenner, and the captor of the biggest fish of the week would pocket the cash.

By 11am the sun and wind had removed all of the ice, and the lough was ready for us to fish. Within an hour of casting out, we were witnessing a site all predator anglers dream of - the area we were fishing was alive with rolling pike. They were everywhere we looked, and to this day I have no idea what caused so many of them to be there. Was it the abundance of food fish such as roach in attendance, or could it have been that they had congregated for spawning? I honestly don't know, but there were hundreds of them.

In the same way that the freezing overnight weather and ice cleared on each day that we were there, so we witnessed this phenomenon repeat itself, too. And, as you would expect, we caught plenty of fish.

The only thing that did change was that as the week progressed, the pike moved further away from the bankside, which meant rowing baits out greater and greater distances. On one occasion I rowed a whole mackerel 150 yards out into the lough, and as I started my return to the bank, one of the lads shouted for me hurry up, because it had been picked up already! I rowed back as fast as I could and was rewarded with a fine 19-pounder.

It was, at the time, one of our best week's piking in Ireland. I was winning the wager with a fish of 26lb right up until that little squirt Marsden took one of 29lb in the last hour before our departure. Jammy git!

It was a fantastic fishing that produced 14 twenties and we lost count of the number of doubles, many of them in the high teens.

It took until winter of 2010 before I decided to revisit the water. What greeted me left me shocked and saddened. By now it was being heavily fished, many of the anglers being of Eastern European origin. I feared the worst. I have seen what can happen to fish stocks when anglers who insist on killing and eating what ➤

PICTURED RIGHT

Rich with a 24lb 4oz fish. Irish winters can be harsh (middle) and the note left on my windscreen by a coward who clearly wanted us off the water.

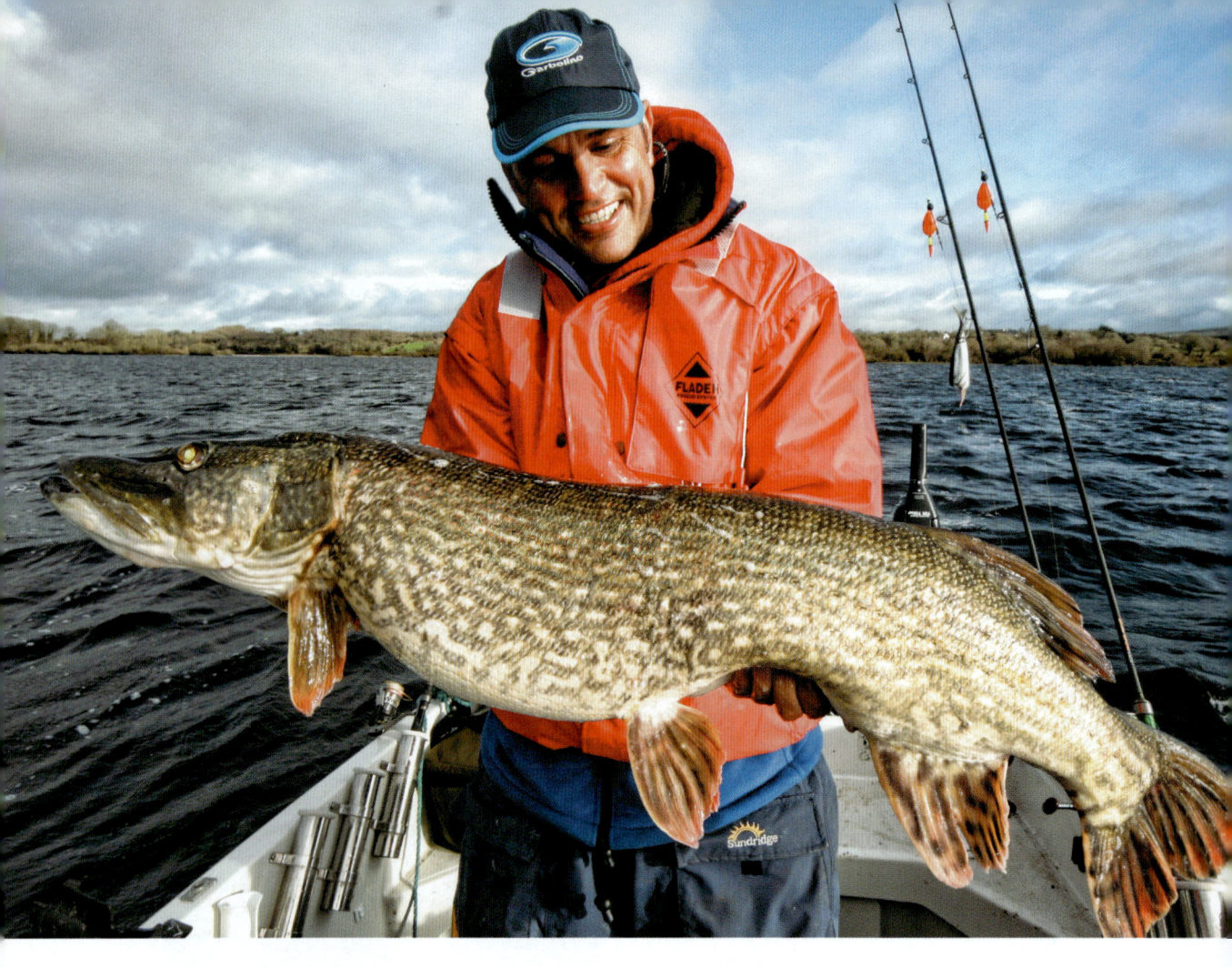

they catch descend on a water.

When will they learn? If they choose to live in another country, they should expect to abide by the law of the land, including the rules relating to the removal of fish. But these guidelines are systematically ignored.

I know that there are bigger and more important problems in the World than illegally taking fish, but we need to look at the bigger picture. Jobs and local business such as hotels, pubs and tackle shops suffer financially if the fishing is poor, and with more and more Eastern Europeans arriving in Ireland and England, the problem is only going to get worse. I urge all Governments, local authorities, clubs, and anglers, to act now to protect our fish stocks before it is too late.

But enough of the politics. As I said earlier, the lough is made up of three sections, all of which are connected by a small river, and I hoped that not many anglers would have bothered with the furthest two. Bank access is severely limited on these parts of the lough, with a boat essential, and the local angling clubs also keep a close eye on the water to deter any illegal activities.

From 2010 to winter of 2012/13, The Gang and I fished the lough on a number of occasions and the results were pretty good. We all caught a few 'twenties' and a good number of reasonable doubles, so it seemed as if the pike population was still healthy, and with no Eastern European interference, it

> **PICTURED ABOVE**
>
> A superb picture of Rich with another mid twenty. At times the fishing was out of this World.

A PIKING OBSESSION
THE SCALES DON'T LIE

was certainly worth more attention.

In November 2012 The Gang and I, without Rich this time, returned to the water for what turned out to be a very special week. The weather wasn't good. It was often raining, with gusty winds blowing from the north, but undeterred we made a start. There are two areas of the lough that have deep water - depths go to 50ft-plus - and these had been fertile ground on previous occasions, mainly because there always seemed to be a lot of resident food fish showing on the fish finders.

Over the next few days I concentrated my efforts in the 20 to 30ft depths with baits such as mackerel, herring, and smelt. I wasn't experiencing what you would call fast and furious action, more steady sport, but what was noticeable was the average size of the fish.

Most were between 16lb and 20lb, with only one jack pike. It seemed almost inevitable that the larger inhabitants would soon make an appearance, and boy did they do it in style! On the third day I landed three 'twenties', at 23lb, 25lb 14oz, and my Irish PB of 28lb 8oz, while Steveo and Phil, who were fishing near me, also had a low 'twenty' fall to their boat.

I made a quick 'phone call to Ugly and The Big Fairy to come and join us. They were fishing the other deep hole in the lough, but the response I got was a little unexpected!

"Move? Bollocks to that!" said Ugly. "We're staying put!"

It turned out that The Big Fairy had taken a fish of 26lb 4oz, and Ugly had really hit the jackpot with a beauty of 31lb. The list of 20lb-plus fish grew by the day, and we still caught some good-sized back-up pike, too. It was simply a great week's fishing. In the end, the top line statistics read: 16 over 20lb and the 31-pounder. Ugly led the way with five of those 'twenties' and the 'thirty'; The Big Fairy had six over 'twenty' to 26lb 4oz; I had five over 'twenty' to 28lb 8oz; and Phil took a 25-pounder.

The following February The Big Fairy, Rich and I were back on the water. We knew it was highly

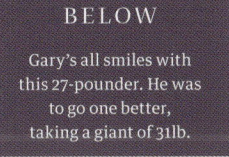

> **PICTURED BELOW**
> Gary's all smiles with this 27-pounder. He was to go one better, taking a giant of 31lb.

A PIKING OBSESSION
THE SCALES DON'T LIE

unlikely we would duplicate the previous November's bonanza, but we still arrived full of confidence, and were not disappointed. The Big Fairy had three over 'twenty', the best 25lb 4oz; Rich had one at the same weight; and I had one of 25lb 14oz.

However, there was a very dark cloud that was to hang low over the trip that left all three of us in real shock and threw doubt on whether we'd ever revisit the country we had come to call a second home. Let me explain.

Mid-way through the week we returned to the boat launching area where our cars and trailers were parked. Rich was first to the vehicles and under the windscreen wipers of each car was a white envelope. On inspection, The Big Fairy found his contained a spent high velocity bullet shell, while mine had exactly the same, together with a note that had ' 1 Warning' scribbled in red ink.

> **PICTURED ABOVE**
>
> The week kept on producing big fish! This one went 25lb 14oz. Look out for the lads in the back of the picture. Naughty boys!

To say we were utterly shocked would be an understatement. That night back at the digs, our conversation was dominated by the discovery. Why would anybody want to issue three anglers with what we perceived to be death threats?

Ireland's recent history meant that our discussions included possible paramilitary involvement, but this was duly dismissed. I don't doubt that the perpetrator was preying on those fears. In the end we all agreed that it was probably nothing more than a jealous and very sad angler who had heard of our recent fishing successes.

There was, in our minds, one clear suspect. It was somebody we had met on the water on previous trips and we all had the same view of him, which was that he was very protective of the fishing on the lough and resented anybody else being there. He acted as if he owned the place, which annoyed me more than the rest of the group because I had first fished there many years before he had ever put in an appearance.

We agreed to inform the local Garda of the threats, mainly to see what their thoughts were, and to see whether any investigative action could be taken. It was with some surprise to us that they took the threats very seriously and vowed to bring the culprit to justice.

A couple of months after our return from Ireland I received a 'phone call from the Garda informing me that they were making some progress in their investigations. They had interviewed two possible suspects, and one of them was about to be DNA tested.

Further months passed before I was contacted once more, this time to tell me that one of the suspects had been fingerprinted but, despite the DNA test, the results were inconclusive. I was told a hand-writing test had also been done.

Then came the bad news. Two weeks on I got another call from the Garda. Although the hand-writing test had shown that there were some similarities between the writing on the death threat note and the suspect's, without conclusive proof, the case was too weak to continue with it.

To say I was disappointed would be an understatement. For the benefit of all anglers and decent people who visit the water, I wanted this person locked up. His cowardly actions have absolutely no place in civilised society, let alone fishing, and the World would be a better place without idiots such as this.

If the perpetrator happens to read this book, I say this to him: if you've done it once, you've probably done it before, and one day you'll be caught in the act. I just hope that pleasure falls to me.

WET, WILD AND HAPPY!

When you're catching fish like this one at 25lb 8oz, you don't mind getting battered by the weather.

A PIKING OBSESSION

THE SCALES DON'T LIE

A MAGICAL RIVER

Targeting the Wye has provided me with a whole new challenge. I've loved trying to understand and master its moods.

PAGE 105

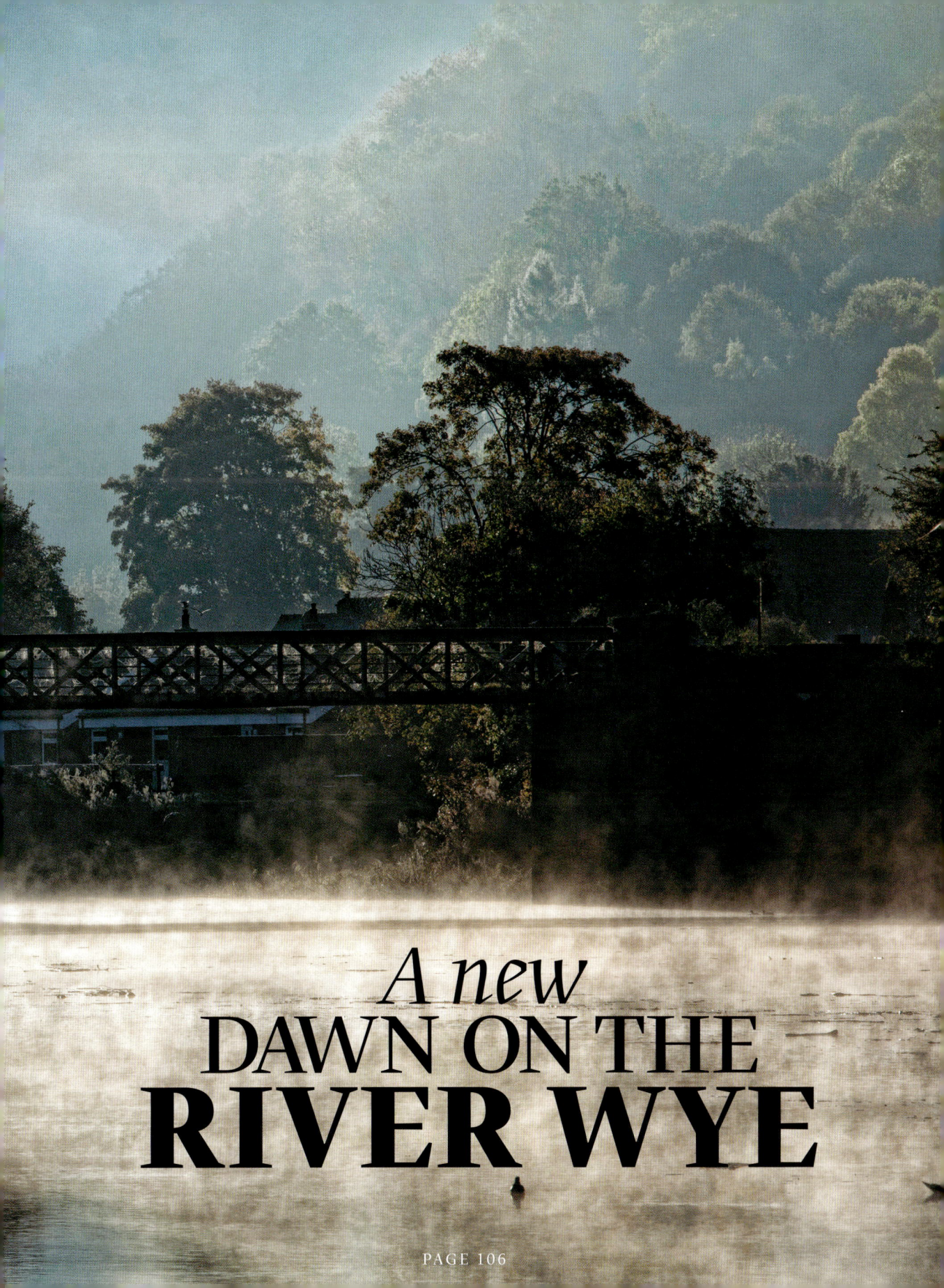

A new DAWN ON THE RIVER WYE

THE BIGGEST YET

This 27lb 4oz pike is the best I've managed so far from the Wye. In truth, a river thirty would be my idea of piking Utopia.

A PIKING OBSESSION

THE SCALES DON'T LIE

In the late '90s, I probably made the best decision of my pike fishing career, which was to explore the River Wye valley. On my very first visit to this truly lovely waterway, I was overcome with emotion at its size and its beauty. I wondered just why I had left it so long before deciding to give it a go.

The Wye has all the right ingredients to produce large pike: it boasts good stocks of fish such as chub, dace, roach, trout and a massive run of migratory shad, of which there are hundreds of thousands in the river from April. It's also far from over-fished, apart from a few well-known areas near Hereford and Ross-on-Wye.

The first few years I spent in the valley were very challenging. As a spate river, water levels can fluctuate dramatically and the overgrown nature of many of the banks makes exploring very difficult. The two-hour drive from my house to the Wye were often wasted journeys, high, coloured water greeting us upon our arrival, and unless you knew the river well enough to fish areas and swims in these conditions, which at the time I didn't, the chances of catching pike were very slim. Blanks were all too numerous.

It was obvious that it was going to take time to get used to the river. I'd need more access to stretches, which meant lining the pockets of farmers, clubs, and syndicates. I would have to chart as many pools, overhanging bushes and snags in the river as I could - all of the likely areas that would hold pike.

I was also fishing the river in summer for barbel and chub, as well as for salmon in the ▶

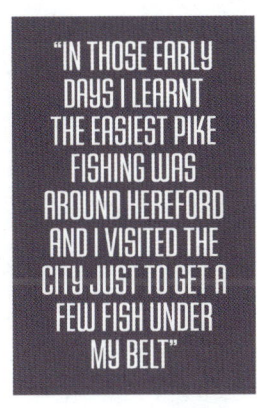

> "IN THOSE EARLY DAYS I LEARNT THE EASIEST PIKE FISHING WAS AROUND HEREFORD AND I VISITED THE CITY JUST TO GET A FEW FISH UNDER MY BELT"

UNTOUCHED BEAUTY

The Upper Wye is a magnificent place to fish. These reaches are, in my opinion, the most beautiful of all.

PAGE 108

coarse fishing Close Season. All the time spent walking the river in pursuit of other species proved hugely valuable in finding likely pike fishing spots for the winter.

Although my success was limited in those early days, it wasn't without the occasional highlight. Travelling such distance from home meant most trips would end up being two-day sessions or more... that's if I could escape from my business commitments

I learnt in those early days on the Wye that the easiest pike fishing was around the Hereford area. I visited the city just to get a few fish under my belt, but I would also always spend a day or two being adventurous and searching new sections of river.

In and around Hereford I was catching a double or two on most visits - the best at this time went 18lb, from the town centre. One day up river on a new beat I was accompanied by a friend of mine - Alan Bassnet - who was on his first Wye pike fishing trip.

I had recently joined a local fishing club that controlled the fishing rights on two miles of water down river from Hay-on-Wye, and the stretch had all the right ingredients to hold big pike. There was also the added advantage of plenty of bankside cover, and a number of trees that had fallen into the river created some perfect ambush spots for predators to strike unsuspecting prey. A couple of previous visits had produced some encouraging results, and I'd landed a few fish to 17lb, but nothing could have prepared me for what was about to happen on that trip with Alan.

The first cast of the day put a whole mackerel

> **PICTURED ABOVE**
>
> The roach shoals move into Hereford town centre as the weather cools and this attracts predators in goood numbers.

A PIKING OBSESSION
THE SCALES DON'T LIE

in the perfect location at the side of one of the fallen trees. Less than an hour later my bobbin fell off the line and rattled my rod rest, and I was out of my chair like a rocket, pulling the hooks into a decent pike. The shock of feeling those barbs hit home caused the fish to leap a couple of feet into the air in a spectacular show of strength and power. My heart missed a couple of beats. This was a man's fish and certainly in the size bracket I had been looking for.

A few moments later I had managed to slide the net under a perfectly conditioned and very long Wye pike that pulled the scales down to 27lb 4oz. I was over the moon. This was my PB for the venue and I was a step closer to achieving my ambition of catching a river 'thirty'.

After Alan had done the business with the photographs, he was soon on his way back to his swim, the words 'that's what a proper pike looks like!' ringing in his ears. You would think that after all the years I've been an angler I'd know better than to take the mick out of somebody when I've just had a good fish. So often it comes back and bites me on the arse - and this was to be no exception.

About an hour after returning my fish to the river, I was close to being in the Land of Nod when I was roused by Alan's voice.

"Do you want to see a 'proper' pike?" he asked.

I couldn't believe it. There in his weigh sling was another Wye biggie, this one at 28lb 6oz. It was a PB for Alan, taken on his first visit to the venue. Sometimes there really is no justice in this World!

All joking apart, I was chuffed for him - I

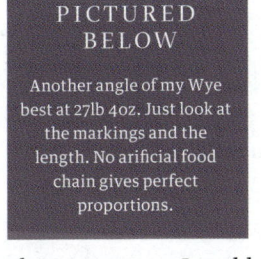

> **PICTURED BELOW**
> Another angle of my Wye best at 27lb 4oz. Just look at the markings and the length. No arificial food chain gives perfect proportions.

PAGE 110

A PIKING OBSESSION
THE SCALES DON'T LIE

> "BY 2008 A PICTURE WAS BEGINNING TO FORM. I CONCLUDED THAT IF I WERE EVER GOING TO CRACK THE WYE, I WOULD NEED MORE HOURS ON THE BANK"

just regret winding him up because for the rest of the day I was the one on the wrong end of the mickey-taking!

As you can imagine, my expectations were sky high for future trips to this particular area of river, but typically of the Wye, just when you think you have it cracked, it comes back to remind you who's boss. I have fished the stretch many times since that day in 2000, and although I've taken many doubles, I haven't had another 'twenty' from there.

For the next couple of years, Hereford was my main focus. For some reason, during the winter months massive shoals of roach and chub invade the town centre stretch of the river. The locals reckon it's down to spawning, and although I can't vouch for that, what I do know is that when they do arrive, the pike are never far away. If you can catch the river conditions right, sport can be awesome. My best from there is 25lb 13oz and I've had numerous quality back-up fish, too.

The only real drawback to the town centre area of the river is the amount of human traffic - at times it is like the M6 on a Friday. On top of that, you have to contend with a lot of inconsiderate rowing boats that will not stay in the middle of the river, but insist on moving along the margins, wiping your lines out as they go past.

By 2008 a picture was beginning to form in my mind. I concluded that if I were ever going to crack the Wye, I would need to spend a lot more time on the banks. With my retirement just around the corner, I started to plan for the future, increasing my club and syndicate

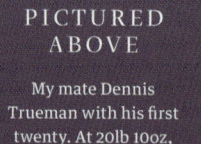

PICTURED ABOVE

My mate Dennis Trueman with his first twenty. At 20lb 10oz, it's a fish he'll never forget.

tickets so that I now had around 20 miles of river to fish. The next part of the plan was to find my own accommodation in Herefordshire - somewhere I could stay for most of the year and that would give me quick and easy access to the river.

With the support of my wife, who understands my love of fishing in the area, we managed to purchase a holiday home on the banks of the River Arrow, in a village called Eardisland. Being just 15 minutes from the Wye, it provided the perfect location, and was not chosen, I hasten to add, because of the two local pubs, full of fantastic people, including a couple of new fishing friends - Dennis Trueman and Ken Fryer.

The third part of 'Plan Wye' was to purchase a good 4x4 Land Rover. This would give me greater access to the river in winter, when the fields become very wet and sometimes treacherous. Buying that vehicle turned out to be one of the best moves I ever made, and not just because of its all-terrain ability. Frankly, it saved my life.

I was fishing on one of my favourite beats, upriver from Hereford, and after blanking in the first couple of swims I decided to move half a mile downstream to some banker swims that almost always gave me a few fish. However, there was a single risky area that I had to negotiate first.

The track was high up from the river, and at one point a large fallen tree partially blocked the way. Opposite, the bank sloped sharply down to the waterway. I had travelled the route numerous times in summer, safely ➼

PICTURED ABOVE

Another Hereford town centre fish. This one went 25lb 13oz. My quest for a Wye thirty continues to this day.

A PIKING OBSESSION
THE SCALES DON'T LIE

> "A CIGAR LATER, I HAD CALMED DOWN ENOUGH TO ASSESS THE SITUATION I WAS NOW IN. I WAS PERILOUSLY CLOSE TO THE DEPTHS OF THE WYE..."

negotiating the tree without an issue, but with all the recent wet weather, the ground was sodden. I should, of course, have got out of the Land Rover and checked the terrain. However, I didn't, and when I was half-way around the tree, the Land Rover started slipping sideways down the bank, only finally coming to a halt on an area of ground the size of the top of a snooker table.

I was metres from the river (and perhaps an early grave). Never have I moved so fast from a vehicle, scrabbling up the bank to safety. I stood shaking on the spot for ten minutes or more.

A Hamlet cigar later, I had calmed down enough to assess the situation I was now in. I was miles from anywhere or anyone, stuck on a small shelf perilously close the depths of the Wye. To the rear of the car was a very wet and steep bank climbing to a height of 15ft, but it was the only possible way out. After 15 minutes or so, with the car door open for an emergency bail-out, I managed to turn the Land Rover around so that it was facing up the slope. I was far from out of trouble, but at least now I had a chance of making it up a very wet gradient.

The chief problem, though, was that each attempt could lead to the vehicle sliding closer to the water. With the door open and my heart

PICTURED ABOVE

The length on this 19-pounder is unbelievable. It has the frame of a much bigger fish but the daily toil of living on a fast-flowing river takes its toll.

in my mouth, there was no other choice but to go for it. Four tries later I was feet from the river and in real trouble. I honestly believed that I had one last chance before I had to bail out and leave the Land Rover where it was and walk.

So, with all the car's off-road controls in place, my foot went down hard on the accelerator and I shot up the slope like a rocket. I went up so fast, I was sure the two front wheels were off the floor! I was up and safe. The relief that washed over me was overwhelming, and at that point I swore the vehicle was worth every penny I'd spent on it. I also vowed to be far more cautious around the banks of the Wye in future.

> **PICTURED ABOVE**
>
> My buddies on the Wye. They shoulder complete responsibility for the size of my beer gut. Boy, do this lot like a drink!

I was by now well into my retirement, and the last few years' piking had been superb. All my planning had gone well and the numbers of doubles and twenties were increasing each year. At the time of writing, I have just put the pike rods away at the end of winter 2012/13, and it turned out to be my best year so far on the Wye, with five 20lb fish. The best went 24lb 1oz and was backed by 62 doubles, many of which were in the teens.

The only disappointment in the past few years has been the fact that my venue best has not gone above 27lb 4oz. But I feel sure one day I'll crack it. If I don't, it won't be for the want of trying.

YOU BEAUTY!

After 60 years of fishing, and thousands of miles travelling across the UK and Ireland, I finally had my big girl - all 43lb 13oz of it!

PAGE 115

A PIKING OBSESSION
THE SCALES DON'T LIE

MY DATE WITH DESTINY

Ever since I caught my first pike at the age of 12, I have dreamed of catching 'the biggest'. For well over half a century I never faltered in my pursuit. I travelled from the wild heathlands of Scotland to the Beacons of Brecon, covering thousands of miles during that epic adventure. Hundreds of waters have been fished, including intimate Highland tarns and vast Irish loughs, all in my search for what I believe is the perfect predator.

However, the truth is that during that journey only a handful of the venues I've fished ever held the potential to deliver a real monster. By 'monster', I mean a pike in excess of 40lb.

All pikers dream of a creature that big, but they are normally more myth and legend than

A PIKING OBSESSION

THE SCALES DON'T LIE

reality. With only 121 authenticated pike over the magical 40lb barrier having ever been caught from the UK and Ireland in the past 50 years (statistics courtesy of Neville Fickling's latest edition of Mammoth Pike), trying to catch a fish over that weight would require a unique formula built on inside knowledge and luck… a lot of luck!

It was March 2011, around midday if memory serves me correctly, and I'd just gone into the garage to stack a delivery of deadbaits for the freezer. The mobile rang. It was Rich.

"Have you heard about the pike?" asked Rich, referring to the out-of-the blue capture by Wyndon Coole of a 45lb 11oz giant from a little-known Yorkshire trout water called Wykeham Lakes.

"Yes," I replied, "I've just seen it in Angling Times. Awesome fish. What do you know about the venue?"

"You're about to find out," said Rich. "We've been invited to fish it for a couple of days. Pack your toothbrush!"

This was a once-in-a-lifetime opportunity. The size of Wykeham - the trout pool is only seven acres - stacked the odds in our favour. We knew that wherever we cast, we'd never be that far away from the pike.

It also hadn't passed me by that the big girl could actually be heavier next time she was caught. When Wyndon had banked her, the fish was just 18oz off the British record. An extra meal or a build-up of weight prior to spawning might put her past the magic milestone. Rich, though, thought I was in cloud cuckoo land and told me to see sense.

"The reality is the pike has just been out, so the chances of catching it again are slim," he reminded me. "I'm there to get some pictures, shoot a film and report on the place. Yes, we'd be mad not to cast out a line, but the most important thing is to nail a feature on the history of Wykeham."

Fair enough, I thought. As long as there was a rod in the water, there was hope, and that was good enough for me.

I counted the days down to the Wykeham trip. Each 24 hours seemed like a week. When the time finally came for me to leave my holiday home in Herefordshire and drive the five hours to North Yorkshire, I kept replaying things over in my head. I was well aware that she'd just been caught, and I knew Rich was there primarily to work, but I just couldn't help but think we had a chance. I sped through the lanes and arrived at the water at a similar time to Rich. We were staying at a local hotel, but decided to catch a glimpse of the water before sunset.

It soon became obvious why the lake had produced such an outsized pike. It was teeming with trout, which were everywhere we looked. With such a high stocking density, every day must have felt like Christmas to an apex Esox. The availability of a boat and as many trout livebaits as we required was a massive plus, as was the fact that we had the place to ourselves. The odds were getting better and better.

Over a good meal and a couple of pints in the local pub, we discussed tactics. We both

PICTURED BELOW

A diet of trout has allowed the Wykeham pike to grow to large sizes. I was lucky to get a second bite after losing the big girl once.

PAGE 117

THE LURE OF TROUT

Our boat was tied up to the trout cage and my bait was positioned just feet from the end.

agreed that having never fished the lake before, we needed to cover as much water as possible, so float trolling our livebaits slowly from area to area would be our first choice. Maybe one would pass close enough to the big girl and tempt her to strike. After a near sleepless night, we were up at first light. There wasn't a second to waste.

Following a crash course in how to use Rich's brand new video camera (I had to know what to do just in case he had the big girl), we were soon afloat, our baits searching out the depths and features of the lake. But nothing happened. For five hours.

It wasn't a massive surprise - the owner had told us that there were very few resident pike - yet, somehow, I couldn't help but feel a bit disappointed. By now our livebaits had covered all of the deep water a number of times with no success, and we felt it was time to try the margins where the shallow water made it impossible to troll our livebaits.

There was one area in particular that had caught our eye. Right next to one of the trout holding cages the fish activity was greater than anywhere else on the lake. We surmised this was probably due to the fact that the owner was regularly feeding the stock in the cages, with some of the pellets falling through and attracting large numbers of trout. It was, therefore, the perfect spot for a large pike to ambush its prey.

After tying the boat to the side of the trout cage, our baits were soon cast to the edge of the deeper water, and we sat back to await any action. The number of trout swimming around and under our boat was amazing, and when we threw pellets into the water the surface would erupt, resembling a Jacuzzi as fish fought to feed. This activity would surely be

HITTING THE JACKPOT

What a stunner. Here she is in all her glory. I know I'll almost certainly never catch anything as big again. I was holding history.

of interest to pike.

It was mid-afternoon when my float suddenly slipped away and disappeared from view. My reactions were sharp - I grabbed the rod firmly in my hand and concentrated my mind. I hesitated to strike, not fully convinced that it was a pike, thinking perhaps one of the very large trout that had been swimming by our boat was responsible. Could it be one of those that had grabbed my livebait? I asked Rich for confirmation.

"What do you think?" I asked.

"Don't take a chance. Hit it!" he replied.

The words had barely finished coming out of his mouth when I struck hard.

"It's on," I shouted. "And it's a pike - look at it, it's huge!" I remember screaming as I caught a glimpse of a giant flank in the clear water.

Then everything went slack. Neither of us spoke. The boat fell into deathly silence as I held my head in my hands. I was utterly distraught. It felt like ten minutes had passed before I finally looked up and said to Rich: "F*****g hell, I don't believe that! The fish of a lifetime and a possible British record and I've just lost it!"

Rich didn't reply. He knew better. I was best left alone to gather my thoughts.

We were still in a sombre mood when we reached the pub. Instead of us celebrating, we were drowning our sorrows, and I was going to finish the bottle of brandy even if it killed me. The evening was hard for both of us, especially when the hotel staff or the local drinkers asked how we had done. No matter how many times we relived it, it didn't numb the pain.

We knew, though, that we had to pull ourselves together. Somehow we had to lift our spirits - our adventure wasn't over yet and we had another day to right the wrongs. But despite our best efforts, we both knew deep down that realistically our best chance had

A PIKING OBSESSION
THE SCALES DON'T LIE

gone. The big girl had been pricked by one of my trebles, and the chances were she wouldn't want to repeat that experience in a hurry.

Dragging myself out of bed the next day with the biggest hangover I'd had in years wasn't easy, but it had to be done. One more day, one more chance and that would be it.

We were soon tied up to the cage once again and our baits were in the same spot as the day before. For the next four hours we sat there watching our floats silently, the only movement coming when they made a bid for freedom. It was eerily quiet, and there was no sign whatsoever of the big girl. Time was moving on and our hopes were fading.

Rich then began having trouble with one of his livebaits. As he was bringing it to the side of the boat to recast, he noticed the trout had tangled on the lead, something which can happen when using live fish. He was standing up in the boat attempting to untangle the mess, the trout still swimming around just under the surface of the water, when there was suddenly a very aggressive snatch that almost ripped the line from his hands.

"Bloody hell," he shouted, "something has just pinched my bait!"

After a few minutes or so of discussing the incident, we both agreed that it must have been one of the large trout that were swimming around our boat. There were lots of them and it seemed to be logical. But the more I thought about it, the more it didn't really make any sense. Our livebaits were a bit too large for even a monster trout to handle, even though sometimes predators do have eyes bigger than their bellies. No, I convinced myself, this might well have been down to the big girl.

It was then that I decided to act. I got one of my livebaits as close to the boat as I could, adjusting my float to the 5ft depth of water underneath us. The sudden click, click, click that signalled line being taken from the reel set my heart pounding. My float bobbed and then dived under the water, the Baitrunner now screaming as the fish moved away from the boat at a rate of knots.

My hands were visibly shaking as I pulled the hooks home. The shape of a massive pike rolled on the surface of the water, its mouth wide open, its head shaking violently as it attempted to dislodge the hooks.

"Put the bloody video camera down and get the landing net ready!" I shouted at Rich, who had switched to journalist mode as a big story began to develop.

> "MY HANDS WERE VISIBLY SHAKING AS I PULLED THE HOOKS HOME. THE SHAPE OF A MASSIVE PIKE ROLLED ON THE SURFACE OF THE WATER..."

A few anxious minutes later she lay beaten in the net - and she was by far the biggest pike either of us had ever seen. I was a complete wreck. My emotions were running high, and I was still suffering from uncontrollable shakes.

Mike, the owner of the fishery, and some of his friends were soon on the scene and preparing the scales for weighing. I was so emotional I could not look as they did the business. Somebody shouted "43lb 13oz!"... not a new record, but that didn't bother me one little bit.

I believe, at the time of capture, it was the ninth biggest authenticated pike ever taken in the UK and Ireland, and I also believe it was the largest pike ever caught 'live' on video camera. If you aren't one of the 1.3 million who've seen it, visit YouTube and enter 'Terry and Rich big pike' into the search engine and you'll get an idea of its vast size.

I was on a real high. I had achieved my lifetime's ambition - to catch a pike in excess of 40lb.

THE EARLY DAYS

Not a monster by today's standards, but this 19-pounder was considered a noteworthy capture in the 1970s.

THE VIEW FROM BOTH SIDES

THE SCALES DON'T LIE

FROM CARPER TO FISHERY BOSS

This section of the book was always going to be the hardest part for me to write about because my feelings about carp fishing have swung in many directions since the capture of my first mirror back in 1970. Today, carp fishing is extremely popular, perhaps the most popular type of fishing, but 40-odd years ago there were very few waters around that held the species, let alone to specimen size. However, these days they seem to be everywhere you go, from ponds, lakes and canals to rivers and reservoirs - you name it, they are resident, such is the demand.

My first carp weighed 11lb and was caught on floating crust from the famous Cuttle Mill fishery, near Tamworth, in the Midlands. To say that I was impressed by the fighting qualities of that first encounter would be an understatement. After watching local anglers catching even bigger, jaw-dropping carp to over 30lb, I was well and truly hooked - I just had to have a lot more of this.

It wasn't long after that first trip to Cuttle that I was proudly sitting at the side of my new carp rods, with two shiny Heron bite alarms and a new 40-inch landing net. I had almost no experience at catching big carp, but with all the new fishing gear, at least I felt as though I knew what I was doing... does this remind you of the youngsters of today? The sound of my first run on my new alarms was one of those moments in angling that will stay with me forever.

IN THE NET

Landing a fish back in the Bigmore days. Carp fishing was very much in its infancy when I started and we had to learn as we went.

There were no Baitrunners in those days to help avoid having your rods dragged into the water, so the reels always had to be set on backwind. There were also no special carp baits sold in shops like there are today. The choice was fairly slim and largely centred around floating bread, luncheon meat, sweetcorn and tinned potatoes - a long way from Mainline Cell.

At the time, one or two of the locals who fished Cuttle were experimenting with paste baits made with baby foods and flavoured colourings. Those experiments were promising, with one lad taking nine fish to 22lb while I blanked on luncheon meat and corn. This proved to me that unique paste

THE VIEW FROM BOTH SIDES

THE SCALES DON'T LIE

baits were the way forward.

After that I spent hours trawling the shelves of the local shops for baby milk powders and rusks for my base mix, to the point where the bloke behind the till asked how big my family was! I tried everything, knowing that it was crucial to get my choice of flavouring right. I didn't want to use the same as the other anglers, and run the risk of it blowing before I had the chance to catch my share. I finally settled for Strawberry flavouring, with a touch of sugar to sweeten it and… bingo! I started to catch more and more carp over that first year. I banked up to a dozen in a session… but no fish over the magical 20lb.

It soon became obvious to me that if I wanted a really big carp I would have to put more time in on the bank, and the only way I could achieve that was to take my wife Chris with me. My 'better half' is a diamond and has never moaned about me putting so much effort into my angling.

There was no night fishing at Cuttle, so we purchased a small touring caravan, and with the help of the owner at that time, Albert Brewer, we were able to leave it in his yard. This new base allowed me more hours to fish in the daytime, yet still spend plenty of time with Chris. Most mornings I would cast out the rods and Chris would have a lie-in before making my breakfast, placing it on a stainless steel serving tray and walking it around the lake to deliver it. You should have heard the comments from some of the anglers jealous of the Silver Service treatment!

My sweet strawberry paste was now working

> **PICTURED ABOVE**
>
> My good friend Ken Hulme with a chunky 13lb-plus mirror. Our learning was shared as we attempted to catch bigger fish.

a treat, but I still had nothing over 20lb. It seemed that every other angler on the bank had caught one besides me. One July morning, just after Chris had delivered my breakfast, I asked her to keep one eye on my rods while I had a pee in the bushes behind my swim. Like I said, she was a diamond. Just as I was finishing my 'call of nature', you guessed it, my alarm sounded and as I turned around Mrs Knight was pulling the hook into a fish.

By the time I reclaimed the tackle, the fish was stuck firmly in a bed of lily pads. All the other anglers on the lake started shouting "Give the rod back to Chris! She hooked it!" I was well and truly out-voted, so I reluctantly gave the rod back to the missus, to cheers from the crowd. A few moments later, the fish was out of the pads and in the landing net... a lovely 24lb mirror. I was really gutted for myself, but pleased for Chris that her first ever carp was such a cracker.

I didn't realise it at the time, but the experience and knowledge I gained by fishing at Cuttle Mill was going to change my life for years to come. On some of the quiet sunny days, while sitting back in my chair, I would often think to myself what a perfect life that Albert had built for himself. The banks of the lake were always busy with anglers and it appeared the ideal way of making money and investing in the future. Running a fishery was surely a labour of love. What better life can you wish for than working within a sport that you adore? To own a lake was every angler's dream, and the seed was sown firmly in my mind. I would do anything possible to find my own fishery.

After I stopped fishing Cuttle on a regular basis, I joined a specimen group called the St Helens Freshwater Study Group. Others like it seemed to be springing up all across the country. The idea behind the groups was that like-minded anglers would meet once a month and exchange information on baits, rigs, venues, what they had caught – anything to help each other to catch specimen fish. I thought this was a great idea and I enjoyed ➤➤

PICTURED RIGHT
How the Liverpool Echo reported news of me buying Burton. The headline says it all really...

THE VIEW FROM BOTH SIDES

THE SCALES DON'T LIE

about three years of membership.

Chairman of the group was a chap named Ronnie Pendleton, and members at that time included Tommy Poynton, Dave MacGibbon and Steve Redman - all anglers with lots of fishing experience, especially with carp. It was down to Ronnie that I finally landed my first 20lb carp, after he kindly offered to take me for a night session on a water called Rainford Flash.

The Flash was a small water on the edge of Rainford village, near St Helens, and the group had been enjoying some success with fish up to 27lb. The hot bait was kidney beans, and I hair-rigged two on my one and only trip. In the early hours of the morning the Heron sounded and after a spirited tussle I slipped the net under a 20lb 2oz mirror. It had been a long wait, but it was worth it.

Waters of this quality in the early '70s were a rare find indeed. Being a 'fishaholic', I had now begun my search for personal bests and started to build a library of Ordnance Survey maps looking for new waters. In the mid-1970s a small highlighted line appeared in the ads page of Angling Times stating: 'Lake For Sale on the Wirral'. There was also a telephone number to call.

After a quick exchange with the agents, I was buzzing, as the lake - known as Gorse Covert Burton - was one I had placed top of my list to watch out for. It ticked all the right boxes and was approximately four acres, featured plenty of lily pads, and was in a beautiful location - I could already see my freshly-stocked carp swimming around the pads.

Burton was up for sale by sealed tender to an estate agent in Chester, and by the time I had seen the place, only 14 days remained until the deadline for submission. The next few weeks

PICTURED BELOW

1 Breaking the ice at Burton during a hard winter.
2 Gordon Little (right) and me in the fishery's shop
3 Old school netting!
4 Me and the Burton regulars.

PAGE 125

were frantic, to say the least. All the necessary searches associated with purchasing any land had to be done, raising the money, meetings with solicitors, accountants and the local planning authority all had to be undertaken. I was about to invest the largest sum of money I had ever parted with, so thorough, but hasty, checks had to be done.

The night before submissions had to be in, I had a meeting with my accountant and solicitor to discuss the amount I should offer. Two hours into the meeting and half a bottle of whisky later, we still hadn't decided on the final sum to tender.

My accountant suggested that it was obvious that I wanted the fishery at any cost, so why not put my intended offer up by £2,000 and clinch the deal. I agreed with him, but my solicitor couldn't understand why anybody would want to buy a hole in the ground with water in it. However, he didn't know about my angling passion - he wasn't a fisherman, and neither was my accountant, although he had seen my cash flow forecasts for the next few years and liked the idea.

My tender was submitted on time the next day, and the following weeks were nail-biting, waiting for the result of my offer. It finally arrived a couple of days before Christmas: 'Mr Knight. Your offer for Gorse Covert Burton has been accepted by the board.' It listed the other offers in the letter and, would you believe it, I had won it by £1,500!

Around this time I had started fishing with Ken Hulme, from Newton-Le-Willows, and it was a fishing partnership that was going to last for the next ten years. I first met Ken, and his wife Joan, at a Pike Anglers' Club conference in the Midlands, and from the word go we got on like a house on fire. We both shared the same love for pike fishing in winter, and he also enjoyed a bit of summer carping. We were very fortunate to obtain two membership cards for a club called Elworth Anglers, based near Sandbach, in Cheshire, and one of the waters they ran was Bigmore. Boy, was this a special venue!

The secretary at the time was a true gent named Bill Greenhall, a nicer man I have never met. In my view, it was his influence that brought carp fishing on Bigmore to the forefront. With Bill's help, and a chap named Ian Gambling, we soon learnt all the secrets we needed to catch the carp from this fantastic lake.

One of the key tricks was always to try to fish into the wind. We also noted that the carp had a real love of particle baits. I can recall how we prebaited for a few weeks with my now favourite particle - maple peas - and we fished them on a hair-rig with a running lead. We attached a single AAA shot about six inches above the swivel, and when the fish took the bait, it would feel the resistance of the lead. The fish would then bolt, pulling the hook home, and this method resulted in almost every run going off like an express train.

> "AFTER A QUICK EXCHANGE WITH THE AGENTS, I WAS BUZZING, AS IT WAS A LAKE THAT I HAD PLACED AT THE TOP OF MY LIST TO WATCH OUT FOR"

In many ways this was an early example of the bolt rig, which is now widely available from most tackle manufacturers. I am not laying claim to this idea, which we picked up from other anglers on the bank, as you do most things, but you can see how popular tactics emerge.

The carp fishing was awesome over the next few years, and Ken and I had hundreds of double-figure fish, many of them in the teens, and we both increased our personal bests to over 22lb. But none of us could match Ian, who was catching in excess of 200 doubles a year.

SUMMER GLORY

Burton in all its summer glory. I spent many happy years running the fishery and I'm proud of the standard of fishing we provided.

We never wanted to fish near to him because his bite alarm would keep you up all night!

The maple peas were amazing. As soon as you catapulted them out, the 'plop, plop, plop' of them hitting the water was like a dinner bell; the noise was so distinct, and the fish moved to the sound instantly.

The work on my new lake was by now well underway. We had to remove lots of fallen trees and rubbish both in and around the water, and we also thinned out the smaller fish, replacing these with my first stock of carp up to 19lb. In the removal of those existing fish, I learnt a valuable lesson: never take any notice of promises made by people involved with the purchase, or sale, of live fish. Instead, always insist that all deals are covered by the necessary paperwork. Let me explain.

In my desire to have good stock, I contacted a fishing club, Lymm Anglers, to enquire whether they would be interested in supplying me with any carp in return for some of my silverfish. The response was very positive, and we arranged to meet the next day in the now renamed Burton Mere Fishery's car park, where I showed a club official some examples of the stock that the club could expect to receive for the carp.

A deal was done, and few weeks later, John Graham and club members arrived to net the lake. They were not disappointed! There was approximately 1,000lb of mixed fish, including lots of 1lb-plus rudd, all in prime condition, and they went away very happy.

Twelve months later and after numerous telephone calls, I still hadn't received any carp and I was forced to instigate legal proceedings against the club. Shortly after that I received a 'phone call from the secretary telling me that they would be delivering some fish to me the next weekend. When they finally arrived, I was very disappointed to find they were not carp, but thousands of three-inch rudd and roach. Luckily for them, I had completed the

THE VIEW FROM BOTH SIDES
THE SCALES DON'T LIE

construction of another water called Woodland Pool, so to avoid the hassle of a protracted court case, I reluctantly accepted the fish in settlement.

A few months later I heard that a club official had been found guilty of stealing the club's van and selling it to some gypsies for scrap. Justice was done. The downside to all this hassle over the fish was that a lot of resentment had been built up against me, solely down to the action I had been forced to take. For years, whenever I went near any of their waters, I would be told I was not welcome, and I bet you if I applied for membership today I would still be refused.

Over the next few years, Burton took up a lot of my spare time. My syndicate members and day tickets were rising year-on-year, as was the weight of the carp I had stocked. We now had about ten 20lb-plus fish, with the best a 24lb mirror nicknamed 'Mug', as it was caught on many occasions. What little spare time I now had I spent trying to catch a personal best from Burton, and I eventually achieved it with my capture of 'Mug' at 23lb 8oz.

The standard of anglers fishing Burton at this time was pretty good, and most of them were well behaved. They all had the welfare of the fish in their minds, and the working parties in the Close Season were always well attended. I spent many a night fishing with most of them, enjoying lots of fun and laughs.

We were now in the mid-'80s, and my love of Burton was still as strong as ever. I was very much still living the dream. The addition of two more pools at Burton increased my workload massively, and I took on my first staff to help out. The two new pools, named Willow and Beech, were built for the up-and-coming fly-fishing market, and were stocked regularly with rainbow and brown trout.

About this time, competition from other fisheries was on the increase, and I wanted to keep one step ahead of the newcomers. With that in mind, I decided to stock some small wels catfish into Burton and Woodland pools. As well as offering an exciting alternative for anglers, they would also help keep the large numbers of silverfish down...enabling the cats to grow fat in the process.

As we approached the early '90s, the average weight of carp at Burton seemed to have levelled out. There were still lots of mid-to-high doubles and some 'twenties' to 25lb to keep my members and day-ticket anglers happy, but I felt that it was time to up the ante, so I decided to purchase a small number of larger carp.

> "WE WERE NOW IN THE MID-'80S AND MY LOVE OF BURTON WAS STILL AS STRONG AS EVER. I WAS VERY MUCH STILL LIVING THE DREAM"

After contacting a well-known fishery in the South of England, and transferring £5,000 from my bank account, I managed to purchase three fish weighing 22lb, 28lb and 35lb. These carp were delivered by a chap named Mike, who worked for the fishery owner. My syndicate members were impressed, and as rumours spread, the demand for season tickets also increased.

It wasn't long after the introduction that the 22lb fish was banked, whilst the 28lb mirror got caught once before it was found dead after six months. The largest specimen, at 35lb, was seen on many occasions swimming around the lake, but was never caught.

Exactly 12 months after the fish were introduced, 'Mike' rang me to enquire whether he could purchase some of the lily pads in the mere. He arrived the following weekend and it was while he was removing the pads that, yes, you guessed it, he found the '35' dead.

I never blamed the suppliers for their deaths, and I put it down to carp of this size

THE VIEW FROM BOTH SIDES

THE SCALES DON'T LIE

> **THOSE WERE THE DAYS**
>
> The eel fishing on Burton was excellent and I spent many a night fishing for them. This one, at 5lb, was caught back in 1992.

probably being quite old and that they never properly adapted to their new home. I was still gutted at wasting £5,000, and the big fish especially still haunts me today, but not just because it died.

While it was on the bank and we were looking for signs of what had caused its death, I made a comment about a mark on its side that looked like a bullet hole, which after investigation was most definitely not! But one idiot who was within earshot must have misheard, because he spread the rumour around that, ludicrously, I had shot the fish myself! People still ask me today if I killed my own fish. Angling could well do without idiotic people like that spreading inaccurate gossip.

It took a while, but by the mid-'90s I was ready to consider stocking some more large carp into Burton. I had been in contact with the then manager of a very famous carp fishery near London, enquiring about the possibility of securing some big fish. A few days later he got back to me, requesting a meeting to discuss a batch of big carp that he was bringing into the UK from the Netherlands.

At the meeting I was told the he'd got clearance from all the necessary Government bodies involved in the importation of live fish, and that they would be coming from a farm in Holland. This guy said he was looking for storage facilities on a fishery with a good level of security, which is exactly what we had at Burton. It also helped that our location was far closer to the port at Hull than his water, and after lengthy discussions I was informed that the delivery would be of around 100 fish up to a weight of 30lb-plus.

The deal was that I would receive four of the largest fish for my pools as payment, which seemed a reasonable offer to me, and the two small stock pools that I had would be the perfect place to store the incoming carp. On the day of their arrival I was amazed at the size of the delivery truck - it was not far off an oil tanker, converted to hold a number of different water tanks to provide plenty of room to carry the fish safely.

Awaiting their arrival at the fishery were officers from the Ministry of Agriculture Fisheries and Food (MAFF), the National Rivers Authority and a freelance fish vet from London, all assembled to check on the health of the carp and to ensure everything was in order. The fish all turned out to be commons, bar one mirror, with the biggest 30lb 4oz.

My four fish to 26lb were stocked into Burton, and I also purchased a 'thirty', before the rest were sold on to other fisheries around the country by the lads from London. Within a year this 26lb common had reached just short of 30lb and all was going well. I even took my PB to 26lb 5oz.

However, at the end of that year I had another 'phone call from London enquiring whether I would be interested in a further movement of fish from the Netherlands. As the first delivery had gone well, I didn't hesitate in saying yes. The same deal was agreed, but disaster was looming. I should have smelt a rat as soon as the fish arrived. They were all mirrors to 38lb and, as many carp anglers know, most fish caught in the Netherlands at that time were commons. Mirrors were quite rare.

A queue of buyers started to arrive at Burton, and the fish were sold to very well-known names in the carp fishing world, some of whom I was told later did not possess the necessary paperwork for the removal, transport and

> "OUR FISH WERE AGAIN STOCKED INTO BURTON MERE, BUT IT WAS NOT LONG BEFORE THE FIRST SIGNS OF IMPENDING DISASTER BEGAN TO SHOW"

WHAT A WASTE

The perils of buying fish from abroad was brought home to me when a diseased batch destroyed much of my resident stock.

THE BURTON GANG

Some of the regulars during the '80s and '90s show off the kind of fish the water became famous for.

stocking of live fish around the UK. Sadly, this practice was widespread at that time.

Our fish were again stocked into Burton Mere, but it was not long before the first signs of impending disaster started to show. The carp and the tench became very lethargic and started to swim lazily on the surface. They refused to feed and started to show physical signs of ill health.

MAFF were called to site and numerous samples were taken away for analysis. I have to say, the three-week wait for the results was one of the worst periods of my life. By now I was burning the corpses of fish that I had looked after for many years and had become very attached to, including Mug and another favourite with the anglers, Pepsi.

The other fish that had been sold on had also affected the waters that they'd been introduced to, causing the deaths of many resident carp in a series of venues across the UK. My worst fears were duly realised, and I was informed by MAFF that the fish had the deadly virus SVC - Spring Viraemia of Carp.

There had been a number of outbreaks in that period, both at home and in Europe, and we were told that there was nothing we could do about it. The virus would have to take its course and they would help us monitor the situation over the next couple of years. All fish movements would be suspended until we were once again given the all-clear.

All I could think about at the time was who was responsible for this disaster. Was it my anglers for continually pressurising me for bigger carp? Or was it simply me chasing bigger profits and pushing the boundaries too far? I decided the biggest share of the blame had to be placed with the suppliers from London. It was they who engineered the deal in Holland.

One of the questions I repeatedly asked

THE VIEW FROM BOTH SIDES
THE SCALES DON'T LIE

them was: Did the carp really originate in Holland or, as I now suspected, were they brought in from other countries that were not classed as disease-free? Also, where were MAFF and the fish vet, who had been there for the first visit? As you would expect, I never got any answers, and by now they weren't even picking up the 'phone.

When the dust finally settled, the biggest regret I had over the whole saga was that I never dragged these crooks through the courts. I'm sure if I had it would have been a good deterrent to the many other so-called fish suppliers, farmers or whatever they call themselves who continually flout the laws on fish movement and persist in introducing disease into our stocks.

After those set-backs I decided to refocus and turned by attention to another battle, one that would go on for a good year or two. I was trying to convince the local planning authority of my need to build a house and shop near the fishery to enable me to improve the facilities, management and security of Burton. The first application I submitted argued a pretty strong case and I felt I had a good chance of success. The presentation was based on the ever-increasing numbers of anglers, 24-hour fishing, the high value of the resident fish stocks and general health and safety.

On the night that the planning committee met, I was in the public gallery eagerly awaiting their decision. I'd heard on the grapevine that the planning officer was likely to recommend my application was refused, and if that were to be the case, I wanted to hear on what grounds. However, I was shocked when my application wasn't even discussed, and the committee of approximately 23 councillors had agreed with the recommendation of one man - the chief planning officer.

None of the councillors had even visited Burton - how could they vote on my future without so much as a look at the place? I quickly arranged another meeting with the chief planning officer to discuss my disgust at the way my application had been treated, and I wanted to know why he had recommended it for refusal. He said he could see no reason why I should need a house in a green belt area, and that I could comfortably manage the fishery from my existing house in the local village. I refuted this completely, suggesting that perhaps he could run his office from his home and save the tax payers some money!

> "ONE OF THE QUESTIONS I REPEATEDLY ASKED THEM WAS: DID THE CARP ORIGINATE IN HOLLAND OR, AS I SUSPECTED, SOMEWHERE ELSE?"

Over the next few weeks I bombarded his office with more paperwork in support of a further application. We had another meeting and he informed me that, again, if I submitted another application, he would still recommend it for refusal. I vowed to press ahead. As far as I was concerned the battle lines had now been drawn... I would just have to consider another approach. Over the coming weeks I carefully prepared my case, and out of 23 councillors on the committee, I managed to persuade all of them, bar one, to meet me at Burton to see what I was doing and why the planning approval was needed.

A couple of the councillors were very impressed and said they would try to help resolve the dispute. I was also told that at the next meeting I would be given the opportunity to put my case directly to the committee, but I would only have five minutes to do so. The night of the council meeting was one of the longest and most stressful of my entire life. I knew if I failed this time, the only route left for me would be a very costly appeal that almost certainly drag on for another year.

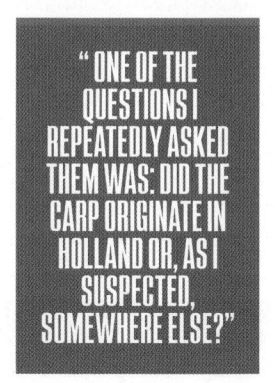

THE VIEW FROM BOTH SIDES

THE SCALES DON'T LIE

But there was also another reason why I needed the decision quickly. I had secretly put an offer in to buy Horseshoe Lake, in the Cotswolds, and my offer had been accepted, subject to me completing the legal side within a one month.

The reason for the secrecy was that the Carp Society were also very interested in purchasing it, so to avoid any possibility of tension between me, the Society, and my own carp anglers, I decided to do all my viewings under the name of Mr Justice (only the agents new my real name). The very first viewing I had was booked under that name, and I arrived at the lake on Saturday morning and met the then bailiff.

"Good morning, Mr Justice. I have instructions to show you around the lake and answer any questions you may have," was his opening gambit. After some discussion it was obvious to me that the anglers who were fishing there at the time knew a potential buyer was visiting the fishery, and my 'disguise' was soon shattered.

"Morning Terry. What are you doing here?" said the first fisherman we walked past.

I realised the cat was out of the bag! In total, six Burton regulars were bivvied up - what a small world angling is. But I digress.

A loud shout of "Yes!" broke the silence in the council chamber after hearing the decision on my planning application for Burton. The committee had gone against the recommendation of the planning officer and voted in favour of my new house and shop at the fishery. I'm sure the celebration could be heard as far away as Liverpool.

> **PICTURED BELOW**
> This old warriior came from Embalse de Chira in the Canaries during a holiday with Chris. It was an adventure I'm never likely to forget!

The only decision to be made now was whether to pull out my offer for Horseshoe Lake. In truth, it was an easy one to make. I withdrew it the very next day; I just couldn't afford to develop both. I sometimes wonder whether it was an opportunity missed, though, because Horseshoe ended up becoming an excellent venue.

Most of my carp fishing in the UK had by now come to an end. I had become completely disillusioned with the scene. Mirrors and commons were being stocked everywhere, and there were a lot of supposed carpers who were barely more than campers. They had all the up-to-date tackle, but little idea of how to use it. Most of them had no experience of fishing for other species, and this often showed when they would accidently catch a fish such as a bream, curse their luck, and if no-one was looking kick it back into the lake. If I had done that with a carp, they would have gone mad, completely ignorant to the fact that if you fish for other species with the proper balanced tackle you can have as much fun as you can carp fishing.

A big part of the sport for me has been the fun of visiting new waters and assessing their big-fish potential for myself. I've found this approach much more satisfying, and I absolutely love big, wild venues that few anglers fish. I don't need the facilities that modern day fisheries provide, largely because I'm always self-sufficient in all my angling. You may think that I am a bit two-faced, having created a very managed world at Burton Mere, and to a point you would be right. But to me Burton was a business, and I provided what my customers wanted, even if I never considered it 'proper' fishing. Apart from an occasional day when I've had nothing else to do, I haven't fished a highly commercialised water for carp since the early '90s, and probably never will again.

I began to focus my attention on carp fishing

PICTURED ABOVE
Embalse de Chria is a remarkable venue and completely different to anywhere I'd fished before. Its depths were remarkable - and so was its carp!

abroad, where I hoped I could find waters that were more suitable and not as regulated as UK lakes had become. On a holiday to the Canaries with Chris I found a water called Embalse de Chira. It was a very large rocky reservoir high in the mountains and seemingly teeming with big carp. I'd heard through the grapevine that the island had a number of lakes that held carp, so I was well prepared when it came to transporting some bait and fishing tackle, despite the limited space available on the plane.

I was sitting in a local bar in Puerto Rico trying to persuade my wife to join me on a carp adventure when a chap called Stuart overheard our conversation. He introduced himself and explained that de Chira was hard to find,

THE VIEW FROM BOTH SIDES
THE SCALES DON'T LIE

but that he knew where it was. He had been an angler years ago and thought by teaming up with me he could join in the carp fun.

Stuart picked us up the next morning and we were away up the mountain. I was genuinely awestruck at my first sighting of the reservoir. The bank areas resembled a lunar landscape, with boulders strewn everywhere, and having no unhooking mats, if I did catch a carp, unhooking it safely would be a nightmare.

I didn't realise it at first, but the reservoir level was up about 10ft after a lot of rain the week before. However, the conundrum of where to start was solved for me when two carp launched into the air right in front of where I was standing! I soon had a bed of sweetcorn and Monster Crab boilies on the lake bed.

I fished two rods with inline leads: one baited with sweetcorn, the other with a boilie. I've found both these baits to be bankers when I've known little about the feeding habits of the resident carp. I was in a world of my own while preparing my swim and tackle, when Stuart shouted: "Bacon butty ready, Tel!"

I couldn't believe it - he had set up a BBQ and the bacon was sizzling away!

On my first cast I seemed to wait an age before my lead found its way to the bottom. It must have been at least 30ft deep - not a depth that I'd choose to fish in, but going by the slopes of the bank, it was probably going to be the norm. By now I had worked out that the water levels in the reservoir were very high, and there was a small bay to my left where I could just see the top of a small tree.

Stuart was sitting by my side, both of us waiting for a take, and it wasn't long before we engaged in a conversation about what he did

HEADING TO FRANCE

This handsome mid twenty came on my very first visit to France in 1993. Chateau de Lorey was the venue in a country I've come to love fishing in.

PAGE 135

for a living here in the Canaries. I was gobsmacked when he told me that he was involved in timeshare apartments, and over the years he had spent a lot of time at 'Her Majesty's Pleasure', serving sentences of up to four years. Apparently he had a daughter back in the UK that he wanted to see more often, but if he returned home, it was likely he would be arrested again. I decided it wasn't a story I would share with Chris!

A screaming run on one of my rods interrupted our conversation and I struck into a proper fish. It powered of to my left in the direction of the partially submerged tree, and within minutes I was up to my neck in water in an attempt to guide her away from the snag. Thankfully I was successful and after a great fight, the fish was in the landing net. At 31lb she was a new best and an incredible introduction to carping in the Canaries.

As the temperature rose, so did the sport, and a further six fish, all doubles, showed a liking for my bait. Stuart and I managed another couple of trips before the missus and I had to fly home, and although we never hit the 30lb mark again, fish to 22lb whet my appetite for more carping abroad.

My next foreign adventure was in France, a country that had featured regularly in the angling press. Famous names such as Rod Hutchinson had done lots of pioneering, catching some very impressive fish for their efforts.

As I had never driven in Europe before, I decided to play safe and organise a trip to a fishery close to the ferry terminal at Cherbourg - a lake called the Chateau de Lorey. It was a very small pool, at half an acre, ideal for a holiday with the wife, while incorporating a little bit of fishing. It turned out to be a fabulous little water that was limited to one or two anglers only, with feature weedbeds and an overhanging tree. It really did feel as if I was on my own Redmire Pool, and I can tell you that the fish I watched swimming around would certainly have been up there with the likes of Clarissa.

On my first night session I had just landed and returned a lovely looking 25lb mirror when I looked down at the floor while tidying up my swim. In the dark, a bright green light appeared, which looked at first glance as if my isotope had fallen out of my bite indicator. As I went to pick it up, it suddenly disappeared! This happened three times before I realised that the swim was alive with glow worms! It was like Blackpool illuminations. Once I'd stopped chasing the glows, I went on to catch another five mirrors over 20lb on that first evening.

> "MY NEXT FOREIGN ADVENTURE WAS IN FRANCE, A COUNTRY THAT HAD FEATURED REGULARLY IN THE ANGLING PRESS. CHATEAU DE LOREY WAS THE VENUE..."

The next night was also very eventful when I had a cracking run on an Activ-8 boilie in the early hours of the morning. As I pulled the hooks home, the fight and feel of the fish was instinctively odd. It didn't take long to get my prize in the landing net, but when my head-torch shone into the mesh, I was met with two big eyes looking up at me and a snarling mess of nasty teeth! I jumped a bloody mile!

Gathering my thoughts, I returned to the swim, but the beast had disappeared. I had a fitful night's sleep before the owner, Andy Short, met me at daybreak. He shed light on my mysterious capture, revealing the 'monster' of the lake to be a coypu, a creature that can grow up to 2ft in length. As Andy walked away, reassuring me that I'd be safe, I had a run on one of my rods, this time resulting in another mint mirror, this one 32lb 2oz - another personal landmark.

THE VIEW FROM BOTH SIDES

THE SCALES DON'T LIE

Burton Mere's new house and shop were by now completed, and the latter was stocked with all the latest fishing tackle. We were bursting at the seams with anglers. However, when I say 'all' the latest gear, little did I realise that some manufacturers would refuse to supply me, claiming that they didn't want to upset local dealers with whom they already had accounts. The problem seemed to be with the reps, and I was told that the angling world was under investigation for illegal activity, though I didn't pursue it as I had other more pressing issues.

All the lakes had been fishing well, the catfish were growing like mad, with a number of them reaching 20lb. We also had a thriving match scene and weights would regularly hit 100lb. And with fishing like that, we regularly had prize money in excess of £1,000. The only problem I had was with the matchmen themselves - they were the biggest load of moaners I had ever come across! Their complaints were numerous and familiar: there were not enough fish; certain pegs shouldn't be used because they were crap; floating baits should be banned - the list went on. These were the most common, but I had more. At one stage they even moaned that some anglers were too good to compete against! No wonder match fishing is on the slide. Who in their right mind wants to put up with that? They kill it for themselves, and it's a problem I've discussed many times with other fishery owners.

French carp fishing was by now well on my radar. Andy Short, from Chateau de Lorey, had started a holiday business with a number of venues on his books. I picked one called

> **FRENCH CARP SUCCESS**
>
> 1 38lb, Rootswood.
> 2 42lb 8oz, Rootswood.
> 3 46lb mirror, Domaine des Iles.
> 4 Big grassie from Metz.

Boulancourt. It was 165 acres, full of large carp, yet there were only eight swims. I loved the sound of it, and I quickly booked all the pegs for the second week of opening.

I was joined on the trip by members of my syndicate at Burton - Les Simson, Richard Smitten, Tony Ward, Ian and Ted Connors, Phil Girling and Ron Erickson - all lads that I got on with well. Over the years I had learnt that when I was going away on a long fishing trip with a large group of people, it was very important to choose the party carefully. One 'bad apple' can cause a lot of problems and spoil the week. After all, it is a holiday, and all I wanted to do is enjoy the fishing and have a laugh.

Boulancourt was also a nature reserve, and they weren't kidding - on the very first day I counted in excess 100 snakes! Fortunately they all seemed to be harmless grass snakes, which was just as well after I found one in my coffee mug! The fishing was hectic to say the least, all of us catching from the off. However, most of the fish were on the small side, with a few barely 1lb, but as the week progressed, some larger specimens did show, and most of us had good doubles, 'twenties' and the a few 'thirties'. I even managed a new PB of 33lb 8oz.

On subsequent trips to Boulancourt the gang continued to catch some good fish, and we were often joined on these adventures by anglers such as my old mates Graham Marsden, Eddie Bibby and others. On one trip I arranged for 42 anglers to fish over two weeks, but the problem was that the group had become too large and some of our invited guests started to create tension among the other members of the party. With me being the organiser, I was often on the receiving end of the moans, the arguing, or whatever else was upsetting individuals. Frankly, I didn't need the hassle, so I soon reduced the group sizes to a maximum of eight.

Over the next eight to ten years I averaged four trips a year to France, and I couldn't get enough of it. I fished on that many waters over there in search of PBs, it just isn't possible to write about them all in this book. If I did, you would probably need a wheelbarrow to carry it. I have thoroughly enjoyed fishing all of these venues, but my two favourites have been Rootswood, near Paris, and The Graviers, near Lyon. But before I fished these two waters, my big fish list had improved and my mirror PB had gone up to 46lb (from Domaine des Iles) together with a 31lb common and a 37lb 8oz grass carp (from Chalet Lake, near Metz).

> "OVER THE NEXT EIGHT TO 10 YEARS I AVERAGED FOUR TRIPS A YEAR TO FRANCE, AND I COULDN'T GET ENOUGH OF IT"

I first fished Sky Lake on Rootswood with my wife, Chris. I managed to persuade her to go for a week's fishing by telling her we could stay in the bivvy at night and she could sunbathe during the day.

The owner at the time was a guy named (yes, you guessed it) Phil Roots, and although he had not had the place for very long, I could tell from my very first meeting with that him he was going to bust a gut to make a success of it. His enthusiasm was almost bubbling over. Although he didn't know for sure the size and quantity of carp in the lake, he was able to describe the fish he had seen or caught in the short time that he had been the owner. The signs were encouraging.

On our arrival at the lake, the first thing that I noticed was how clear the water was. It was like drinking water. You could see every stone, twig or whatever else was on the bottom. But this didn't seem to bother the many large carp I could see swimming and feeding in the margins. As far as I was concerned, this was

THE VIEW FROM BOTH SIDES

THE SCALES DON'T LIE

a good sign - the fish had clearly not seen too much pressure from anglers.

I chose a swim right in the corner of the lake, where a lot of carp seemed to be swimming in and out of a couple of fallen trees. My thinking was that I could put a bait right in the path of the fish as they swam in and out of the snags. I could also put a bait on the far margin, which was only about 50 yards away. I baited up with a small amount of brown groundbait mixed with hemp and a small amount of 15mm cranberry boilies. The trap was now set.

I had set up two bivvies for Chris and me: one was for us to sleep in, and the other for cooking and keeping our food away from any vermin that might have fancied a free meal. It was an ideal set-up, and very comfortable for a week's fishing. I also ensured that both bivvies were positioned well back in the trees, to avoid disturbing any fish that may have fancied feeding in the margins close to us.

The weather was incredibly hot and humid during daylight hours, but at night the storms would arrive... and what storms they were! I'd never, ever experienced lightning like it - huge shards that would illuminate the landscape in spectacular fashion. Then the rain would fall. It was torrential, and we'd leave the canvas shelter for something a bit more substantial - running for the car that was fortunately parked just behind the swim. We'd sit there, a bottle of wine on the go, listening to the almighty din of the elements and laugh our heads off at what our friends would make of our predicament.

One night in a spectacular storm, the carp went crazy and I had six fish to 25lb. I was completely soaked, but with the air temperature so high, I never felt cold, and in many ways it was like having a refreshing shower every time I made a dash for the rods.

The only time I began to worry was when I was playing the fish. Would my carbon fibre rod act as a conductor, and could I be struck by lightning? The answer was, of course, yes, but I guess I played the percentage game and got lucky.

Early one morning after the storms had relented, the rod that was fishing the fallen trees screamed into life. The bait had been taken and I pulled the hook home before the fish powered out of the snags and into the main part of the lake, causing a bow wave similar to a mini tsunami.

It was immediately obvious that this was a very large fish. Thirty minutes later, and after one of the best fights I've ever had from a carp, a 42lb 8oz beautifully-conditioned mirror lay beaten in the folds of the landing net.

Over the course of the week I caught 25 carp, including 21 doubles, three twenties and the aforementioned 42lb 8oz mirror. For a new water, this was a good return, and the fact that I had spotted many other fish that looked much bigger than my 'forty' meant it would not be long before my return.

Not all of the trips to France go well, as I found out on my return to Rootswood. This time I was joined by my long-term angling partner Richard Lee and friend Kevin McLean. When we arrived at the lake I was stunned at what greeted us. As we drove down the approach lane to the lake, we found the 10ft high gates at the entrance completely underwater. It turned out that the River Seine that runs adjacent to the lakes had burst its banks after a recent bout of especially heavy rain.

Fishery owner Phil met us in a rowing boat to transport all our tackle to the lake cabin, which was now sitting on an island and well and truly cut off from the main bank. And as

> **PICTURED RIGHT**
>
> Boulancourt, 1994. This 25lb 8oz mirror was one of numerous quality fish taken on the trip.

we rowed the boat over the swim that Chris and I had fished on my last trip, Phil's echo sounder read 16ft deep! It was looking like a complete disaster. There were, said Phil, no fishable swims at all on Sky Lake, as they were all completely submerged. The water had also flooded through the trees and into the fields behind the lake. To put it bluntly, the place was a mess and we were all gutted.

However, there was a lake of about 80 acres right next door called The Barron. Phil informed us that although the lake was not in his control, the owner was a friend who, given the unforeseen conditions at Rootswood, had kindly offered us the chance to fish it. Although Phil could offer us little in the way of information on how to approach the venue, at least there were a small number of swims that allowed a level of comfort. The only crumb of detail he had for us was that some very large fish had been spotted in the margins and seen crashing around the islands.

With Phil kindly allowing us the use of his boat and the echo sounder, we were able to assess the depths of water around the two islands. We soon discovered that the area out to the islands was very deep, averaging about 30ft, but between the two islands there was a shelf showing a depth of 12ft. It looked the perfect area to start fishing. The distance from the bank out to this inviting area was around 160 metres, way too far to cast or present a decent bed of freebies. It was, therefore, one of those occasions when our bait boats would be invaluable.

Love them or loathe them, without them the trip would have been completely ruined. At Burton Mere I allowed bait boats because

THE VIEW FROM BOTH SIDES

THE SCALES DON'T LIE

HARD TO BEAT

This has to be one of the finest-looking carp I've ever caught. It went 42lb and came from Rootswood in July, 2003.

some anglers were that hopeless at casting, their baits would often land on the island, resulting in line left in the bushes and trees. This was obviously potentially fatal to the resident wildlife. In the right place at the right time they often make the difference between catching and blanking, so I always view them as another tool in my armoury to catch fish.

As we feared, the fishing was dreadful, and all the extra water had really turned the fish off feeding. We did have an occasional fish roll near our swims, but none of us had so much as a liner, let alone a positive take. Frankly, it was a complete disaster. We also had to endure uncomfortable night-times, and on occasions it felt as if we were camped in the middle of Jurassic Park! Whatever was responsible was big, noisy and not something you wanted to bump into outside the bivvy!

The vegetation along the lake side was like a jungle, and walking any distance was hard work. But after a good breakfast with Phil each morning, we made it with some kind of fresh hope for the day. It was on one of these mornings when walking back to my swim that I stopped at a small gap in the bushes alongside the lake. I was looking out to the opposite end of the island where we had been fishing when a large carp rolled right under the bushes and very close in to the island. The distance would certainly necessitate the use of the bait boat, and maybe Phil would allow me to clear some of the vegetation to make room for my bivvy. As we'd caught nothing at the other end of the island, it was certainly worth asking.

By now there was a really strong wind blowing down the lake, with waves about 2ft high and the swim I was about to move into would place me right in the teeth of it. Although it was bordering on too strong, having the wind in my face has always been a favoured fishing position of mine on any lake

- and this was no different. After baiting up my three rods with a bait boat full of hemp and Activ-8 boilies, I settled into my new swim for the night. Fortunately, the wind finally dropped around midnight and I was soon in the Land of Nod.

But not for long. Around midnight I was woken by one hell of a noise outside my bivvy. It sounded like a stampede of wild animals, and one of whatever was responsible hit my bivvy with that much force, it almost knocked me off my bedchair. I can't lie - it frightened the bloody life out of me, and for the next hour or two I lay there and never moved a muscle. It was with some relief that I finally heard them moving away in the direction of Rich and Kevin. When dawn broke I still had the shakes. Night fishing up to that point had never bothered me, but that experience certainly tested my resolve.

After re-baiting my rods and supping a quick brew, my eyes began to shut. The lack of sleep from the previous night was just too much to resist. A short while later I was woken again, but not by the kind of noise I'd experienced a few hours before. Call it a sixth sense, but something made me open my eyes and there, looking directly at me through my bivvy door, was a huge wild boar. It just stood there motionless, its glare fixed on mine.

"Bloody hell! Get me out of here!," I thought. But before I could react, another huge beast walked into view, followed by four smaller ones. A whole flipping family was soon standing about three metres away from me, watching my every move. After what seemed an age, but was probably less than a couple of minutes, they decided I was of little importance and slowly moved on. Boy, was I grateful. The Jurassic Park monsters had finally showed themselves, and the next night I left a small light and a radio on to deter any more visits. It worked a treat and I never saw or heard them again.

With one night of our trip left, and none of us having caught a fish, we were all resigned to defeat. What an unmitigated disaster! However, I am not the sort of person to give in lightly, and the harder it gets, the more determined I become. My spirit was low but not completely diminished, and as I was still seeing occasional fish roll in my swim, I remained hopeful that sooner or later one of them might feed on my bait. The question was, would it happen before our departure for home?

With one hour before are planned time to leave, the indicator on my right-hand rod slammed into the rod butt and, at last, I was able to lift into a fish. It immediately kited to the right of the island and headed into the corner of the lake. The fight was incredible, certainly one of the hardest I have ever experienced, and it just wouldn't give up. Using the advantage of the deep water immediately in front of my swim, it did everything it could to shake the hook free, but I was determined that this battle was going to end with a smile. Forty minutes later I finally had the fish in my landing net. In the worst conditions I had ever fished for carp, I ➡

PICTURED ABOVE
Another French whacker. I can't imagine a time when I won't make the journey. It's a fabulous country and the fishing is largely exceptional.

THE VIEW FROM BOTH SIDES

THE SCALES DON'T LIE

had finished our nightmare trip on a high.

On my first look, I knew it was not going to beat my PB of 46lb, but what a fish! It was a mint-conditioned mirror of 38lb, and as well as putting up an incredible fight, it was vindication for the move of swims and worth suffering my sleepless night at the hands of the wild boars. Rich and Kev couldn't believe it. Both of them were calling me a jammy git - and worse! - and I have to admit that someone must have been looking down on me.

After we had loaded the boat with our gear, we made our way back across the lake towards the car. We'd just passed through the still-submerged entrance gates when we spotted two French anglers who we'd got talking to throughout the week. It was one of the funniest sights I've ever seen. They had opened a field gate that was partially submerged, and were casting their baits through the gate and into the floodwater that was covering a ploughed field! Would you believe it, the area was full of carp. The fish had swum out of the main lake and into the fields! It was no wonder we'd been struggling to catch, as most of the lake's residents had relocated to this area.

The French lads were having a beano, catching lots of carp in the high 'thirties'. Now that's what you call opportunistic angling!

Over the next couple of years or so I fished Sky Lake around three or four times a year in the company of a variety of anglers. Many of them were from the Wirral 'L' Pool and Cheshire area, and quite a few often fished Burton Mere. Between us we had numerous carp in the 50lb region, my best going 51lb. Richard Smitten had one at 53lb, while Gary Caldwell banked fish of 54lb, together with an absolute whopper of a mirror at 60lb. That carp turned out to be the same one I'd taken on my first visit to the venue three years earlier at 42lb 8oz - some growth rate!

During that period we had many memorable trips to Sky, with one week in particular standing out. I had recently purchased a 23ft motorhome, so that my wife, Chris, could join me on my fishing adventures more often, and we parked it between Sky Lake and Barron Lake. Chris stayed in comfort and I took up residence in my bivvy. It was 5-star fishing, with hot meals delivered to my swim every day.

Since that very first trip to Sky, the carp had come under increasing pressure and, consequently, had wised up a lot. By now it was rare to see one swimming in the margins during the day. Instead they seemed to hang out at the furthest distance from anglers. This was bang in the centre of the lake, so I positioned the motorhome in the swim that gave me the best access point. That week turned out to be one of the best I'd ever enjoyed in France, and I landed a total of 33 fish, including a 42lb heavily-scaled mirror, 17 'thirties', ten 'twenties' and five high doubles. And not a wild boar in sight!

In the meantime, Burton Mere was still booming, but my patience with the matchmen was becoming very, very thin. Their petty moaning was relentless, even though I did

> **PICTURED ABOVE LEFT**
>
> The catfishing at Burton came on brilliantly over the years and one man who knew how to catch them was Phil Smith.

everything I could to keep them happy. In my view they had the best match fishery in the area, but they refused to see it. Matters came to a head one weekend. I had a shop full of matchmen waiting to draw for pegs when they began arguing between themselves about which lake the match should be held on. I told them in no uncertain terms that this was my decision, not theirs, and when one or two of them threatened not to fish, that was the last straw. I wasn't going to be held to ransom by anybody. Enough was enough and I informed them that this, and all future open matches, were to be cancelled. Going forward, the match lakes would only be open for club matches and day-ticket sales.

It turned out to be a great decision. I didn't realise the demand for fishing these pools would be so good, and the lakes were full every day, especially in summer. And the other big spin-off was the increase in shop sales. Day-ticket anglers certainly spent more money than the matchmen!

The carp in the other pools were still doing well, but the catfish proved to be something else altogether. They were growing at a phenomenal rate, with some of them now approaching 70lb. There were also plenty of 30lb, 40lb and 50lb fish coming through. During the summer they'd get caught almost daily, and the demand for these hard-fighting predators was overtaking the carp fishing.

During the period I'd been regularly fishing in France, I'd also taken occasional catfishing trips to the River Saone in the company of guide Luke Moffatt. Luke had specialised in catfishing for a number of years and there wasn't much he

> **PICTURED BELOW**
>
> 1 32lb, Chateau de Lorey
> 2 36lb 2oz, Boulancourt.
> 3 Richie Smitten with a 55lb fish from The Graviers
> 4 Gary Caldwell with a 59-pounder, Rootswood.

PERSONAL BEST

My quest for a really monstrous carp continues to this day. This 52lb The Graviers fish is my best to date. I hope to beat it though!

did not know about them. But on our last trip with him I could sense that he was looking for a change of direction, and we spoke at length about the possibility of finding him a carp water in France. A few months later I took a 'phone call from Luke; he'd found a venue near Dijon and he was hoping to open it in the near future.

It was now early in 2000 and I'd made my first booking to Luke's. As with any new water, you are never quite sure what to expect, and although Luke had seen a number of large fish prior to his purchase of the now-named The Graviers, and indeed caught a few in excess of 40lb since becoming owner, it was still something of an unknown quantity. On my first visit I was accompanied again by close friends Richard Lee and Kevin MacLean, and as soon as the three of us set eyes on the place, we loved it.

I didn't know it at the time, but over the next couple of years my affection for The Graviers would continue to grow, and at one stage I even said to Luke that if he ever came to sell it, I would certainly be interested in buying it from him. To me it was the ideal carp lake, the best one I had ever fished, and not just because of the size of fish that would eventually be taken from its waters. It was more to do with the way that Luke ran the fishery. At that time he only allowed a maximum of five anglers on the 20-acre water, and this was heaven to me. As I said earlier on, I love my own company, and if I wanted isolation, I could certainly find it on The Graviers. That's not to say I am a miserable sod, or don't enjoy spending time with friends, because I do, but when the fishing is a challenge, I like to blend in with the surroundings and make my own

THE VIEW FROM BOTH SIDES

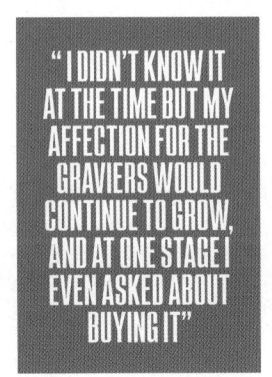

THE SCALES DON'T LIE

decisions on how to catch my quarry without anyone else clouding my judgement.

One of the best things I learned on The Graviers was how to find carp and keep them in my swim. On most trips we would pick our swims by drawing lots for first choice, and I soon learnt that winning the draw was not always for the best. You could sometimes be influenced by what carp had been caught in certain swims on previous visits and, as we all know, for whatever reasons, fish do move about.

One example of this happened on our second trip. On arrival we walked around the lake and spotted a lot of carp in one swim they call 'The Spit'. I should have known better, but in my eagerness to start fishing I never even considered my surroundings.

The swim was horribly exposed, and with the weather for the week forecast to be extremely hot, I was soon suffering. Within a short spell, the fish had spooked at all the bankside disturbance, and to make matters worse, by the second day I felt really ill. It was 'Doctor' Luke who spotted the signs - the extreme heat had brought on dehydration and he insisted I drank a lot of water. In the next hour I downed six one-litre bottles, and soon started to feel better.

I learnt a lot from that experience and eventually found it best to have last choice of swim. My theory being that I'd let everybody else chose first, allowing them to set-up and get comfortable before I made my selection. Why? Often the fish would be spooked with all the commotion, and by being patient I could select a swim as far away from everybody else, in areas where carp might feel safer. Was it successful? Not always, but I certainly felt more confident adopting this approach.

I would also always try to make sure that the wind was blowing into my swim, too. If that wasn't possible, all I could do was hope that over the week it would do so at some point, because I've always found it a big plus. The other thing that I learnt quickly about fishing at The Graviers was that placing my bivvy well back from the water's edge, and ideally under or behind some form of bankside cover, was essential, on two counts. One, it would help protect me from the hot sun, and secondly, coupled with camouflaged netting at my bivvy door, it meant that I was less likely to spook any fish.

When conditions allowed, another good move was dispensing with any hanging indicators, and fishing slack lines instead. This allowed our main line to sink to the bottom of the lake and make sure any carp swimming off bottom didn't bump into taut mono. It certainly wasn't what you could describe as easy fishing in those early days, but it suited my style perfectly. When I caught a fish, I felt as if I'd really earned it.

> "I DIDN'T KNOW IT AT THE TIME BUT MY AFFECTION FOR THE GRAVIERS WOULD CONTINUE TO GROW, AND AT ONE STAGE I EVEN ASKED ABOUT BUYING IT"

Before Luke bought the lake, the previous owners had run a restaurant on its banks, and it had been very popular with the locals, who used it as a place to bathe during the long, hot summers. Apparently they used to feed the carp, which would come looking for an easy meal. One rumour that had us all interested involved the capture of a 50lb fish that the local angler who caught it found had a rope tied around its body. According to those who told the story, the rope had been there so long, the skin of the fish had started to grow around it. When it was removed, a huge scar was visible across both flanks. It sounded far-fetched but, as history would show, entirely possible.

On our very first visit to the lake, Rich said he spotted a large carp that matched the description of the fish in the story, and I don't know whether it was Luke or somebody

THE VIEW FROM BOTH SIDES

THE SCALES DON'T LIE

"IT WAS OBVIOUS THAT HE HAD FOUND SOME FISH TO STALK… MY EYES NEARLY JUMPED OUT OF MY HEAD WHEN I SPOTTED 'THE SCAR'"

MORNING GLORY

France is a special country. I love the vastness and the sense of freedom it offers. And the carp fishing's not bad either!

PAGE 148

THE WAITING GAME

My great friend Rich Lee sets the bobbins as the day dawns on another day in France. We've travelled across together for years and continue to do so.

else who named it, but the creature became known as 'The Scar', and it would go down in angling history. It reached a World record weight of 99lb in June 2010, and ensured that The Graviers would forever be remembered as one of the great carp venues of all time.

We were very fortunate over those early years to follow with great interest the progress 'The Scar', watching it put on weight year after year, and those who were luckily enough to catch it were able to hold the fish of a lifetime.

Neither I, nor my friends, ever caught it, but we came very close on a number of occasions. It was taken from swims I was due to fish just a single day before my arrival on two occasions, but it was Rich who came the closest.

On one trip he was field-testing a new rod from Fox called 'Bonsai'. It was different from conventional carp rods in as much as it didn't have eyes, as the line passed from the reel through the centre of the blank before coming out again at the tip. It had been designed for stalking, enabling the angler to get into heavy undergrowth without the line tangling on branches or vegetation. He had been gone for about two hours when I spotted him under some bushes lying flat on his stomach. He was signalling me to come over.

It was obvious that he had found some fish to stalk, so I crept around on all fours and came in from the back of him so as not to disturb any carp he was after. My eyes nearly jumped out of my head when I spotted 'The Scar' together with a few other large fish swimming around under his rod tip. 'The Scar' was truly massive, and both our hearts missed a beat when his sweetcorn suddenly ended up on its head, before falling off the side and underneath the fish.

After ten minutes or so I crept away, but I hadn't got more than 50 metres away when I heard one hell of a splash and saw Rich neck-deep in the water. It was immediately obvious to me that he was into a fish, so I legged it back to him, grabbing the landing net as the fish charged about 50 metres down the margin. It

THE VIEW FROM BOTH SIDES

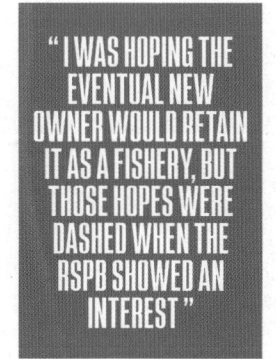

THE SCALES DON'T LIE

was putting up one hell of a scrap, and we both looked at each, not saying a word, but knowing this could be his moment of destiny. A few minutes later a fish of 25lb lay in the landing net. Rich was gutted. He had been so close to a World record and knew his chance may not come again. As it was, 'The Scar' was caught a week later from the swim I had been fishing at 84lb, which, I was told at the time, was a new World best. That's how close Rich had been.

We continued to fish The Graviers for the next few years, going as often as we could, and I pushed my PB up to 52lb with a cracking mirror. However, the most successful of our group was Richard Smitten. The jammy so-and-so couldn't put a foot wrong, and landed three 'fifties' to 58lb and two 'sixties', at 65lb 8oz and 68lb. It was certainly his lucky water.

I was now in my mid-50s and my 30-year love affair with Burton Mere was starting to wear a bit thin. I was very proud of what I had achieved at the fishery, but it was now starting to turn into a monster. I had developed the business into something far larger than I had ever intended, and instead of having more time to go fishing and do the other things we all want to do later in life, it was now a 24-hour commitment. I'd also noticed in the three decades of running the complex that the clientele had changed significantly.

In those early years most of the anglers were more responsible, with litter, noise and vandalism problems infrequent. But the modern angler was much different, and problems became a daily occurrence. There seemed to be almost no respect, especially from the younger generations, and booze and drugs started to a play a major part in destroying the sport I love.

Also, the misuse of mobile phones started to cause us numerous problems. We'd get bored anglers ringing their friends to ask them to bring chips, booze, girlfriends or whatever down to the fishery - often in the early hours of the morning when the main gate was closed. They'd set the alarms off, and when I'd worked a 16-hour day, I was not impressed at having to get out of bed three or four times a night.

As I said, the modern angler seemed to have very little respect for property, other people, wildlife, and even the fish. I was finding it increasingly hard to cope with the problems, and the pressure was pushing me in a direction I never thought I would take.

I've always had the belief that whatever you do in life should be enjoyable, and if it is, you'll do it well. But when the pleasure goes, and it becomes hard work, then it is time to move on. After a lot of sleepless nights, I finally decided my dream was over and it was time for me to sell Burton Mere.

I had worked all my life, but it was now time to go into early retirement and do more of what I enjoyed most - fishing. In the first few months of Burton being on the market we had 60 viewings - a remarkable amount of people, and the interest really surprised me. I knew that Burton was very special to a lot of people, and not all of them were anglers, but this was way above our expectations.

> "I WAS HOPING THE EVENTUAL NEW OWNER WOULD RETAIN IT AS A FISHERY, BUT THOSE HOPES WERE DASHED WHEN THE RSPB SHOWED AN INTEREST"

I was hoping that the eventual new owner would retain it as a fishery, but those hopes were soon dashed when the RSPB (Royal Society for Protection of Birds) started to show a keen interest. Burton was sited on the edge of its existing reserve, and it was short of car parking spaces, so our fishery was ideal.

Less than a year later the deal was finalised, and the RSPB became the new owner. One chapter in my life was coming to an end... but another was about to open.

MAGIC ON THE MERE

This quartet of big bream came from Cholmondeley. Back in those days specimen hunters were thin on the ground and big fish hard to come by.

BIG FISH FROM BIG WATERS
THE SCALES DON'T LIE

CHASING THE BREAM DREAM

It was on my first trip to Ireland that a love affair with bream began. May 1969 was a very special month. I'd travelled to County Cavan with my pal, Mike Jordan, following an article by Ivan Marks in Angling Times. Ivan told a tale of the River Annalee, heralding it as the greatest roach venue of all-time. And he was right - the waterway was paved with silverfish.

But it was during the stay, over a Guinness in the local pub, that we started chatting with a group of holidaying anglers from Chester. They explained that after prebaiting heavily on the River Erne at Killykeen, they'd started to catch bream. But not just a few. Fish after fish had filled their huge nets until they were almost impossible to lift.

We scribbled our treasure map on the back of a beer mat and the next day went in search of the pegs. The directions to the swim were unerringly precise, and even before we could thread the mono through the rod guides we could see shapes rolling in the distance.

At 50 yards the dorsal fins of bream cut through the surface. They looked immense as they porpoised over the baited area. Following the instructions of the Chester lads to the letter, we introduced 20 tennis ball-sized balls of groundbait loaded with maggots in an attempt to hold the fish in the swim. And boy did it work.

Using running leads - this was before the lads on the Severn had invented feeders by adapting hair curlers - bites came from the very first cast and never slowed down until mid-afternoon. By then we were knackered, as most of the fish were in the 5lb bracket with my PB rising to 7lb 3oz. Looking down at our bulging nets we estimated we had landed somewhere between 5-600lb of Irish slabs!

With the bream obsession ignited, I spent the next ten to 15 summers fishing the Cheshire meres - low-stock waters created during the last ice age. Those stocking densities had deterred many traditional anglers, who were mainly on the rivers and canals, and I began to see the same faces - all men driven by the obsession of catching the biggest. With so little charted information, and certainly ➤

BIG BRACE
Marbury Mere provided these two quality bream. We were very much pioneers in those days and trial and error was the only way to succeed.

BIG FISH FROM BIG WATERS
THE SCALES DON'T LIE

no internet to exchange knowledge, we were fuelled by dreams of catching uncaught monsters that in reality probably never existed. Or did they?

Redesmere is a 30 acre-ish water nestling between Congleton and Macclesfield, and it had a track record for bigger than average fish. Rumour had it that bream of over 10lb had been landed from this up-and-coming lake. This was to be my next focal point.

It was one spring evening, whilst feeding my Doberman Pinscher called Bruno, that I started to wonder whether tinned dog food could have a secondary use. For fish! The contents of the Bounce cans had a pungent smell, and the gravy would surely leave an attractive cloud in the water. Couple that with the meaty chunks and you had a recipe for catching fish. Was this to be my edge?

People who know me will tell you that I'm not an advocate of moderation, so after a few 'phone calls I managed to locate 100 tins of Bounce. I think they were technically 'seconds' as the cans had a few dints in them, which would explain the seller's claim that they 'fell off the back of a lorry.' I asked little and paid him the money. Job done.

Trying to decide how to feed gallons of meaty slop was the next problem, so I met with close pal Ian Whitehead to hatch a plan so cunning, no bream could ignore it. We'd mix the meat with brown crumb and ball it into three swims to get the fish familiar with the new bait attack.

For five weeks prior to the season opening we began the bombardment, as we introduced our signature feed. Three days a week we

> **PICTURED ABOVE**
>
> You wouldn't get away with a keepnet like that nowadays! My first trip to Ireland was in search of bream…and we found them!

chucked that stinking concoction into the mere in an obsessive pursuit of a new personal best. Come opening day, the bream would be hunting out our carpet of bait and ignoring everyone else's attack.

June 11, and we set up camp on our chosen roadside swims. Five days of staring at the water and dreaming of giants lay ahead, but we simply couldn't risk turning up the night before and not getting the pegs. Redesmere might have well been a low-stock water, but there were enough specimen fish obsessives in the North West to take all the top spots.

Eventually the watch hands hit midnight on June 16, and out went the rods. The anticipation reached a fever pitch as both Ian and I raced to get a bait in the water. Hookbait choice had been much debated. If we were throwing in a mountain of Bounce, surely the flavour should feature in our hookbait. The meaty chunks were too soft to handle a cast, so we moulded a stiff dog food paste using liquidised white bread.

With the rods in the rests and bobbins clipped on, we waited for the giants to hang themselves. For the next few hours we got run after run, but as dawn broke we were blanking. Five weeks of effort for bloody nothing. The dog food plan was well and truly in the doghouse. The groundbaiting had clearly attracted some fish into the swim - quite what species was still to be identified - so we switched our rigs to simple maggot feeder set ups.

Fishing two rods apiece, we cast the rigs 50 yards into 8ft of water and it wasn't long before the change of attack paid dividends. Within a few hours I'd landed 17 bream to 9lb 12oz. The Bounce experiment had in fact paid off in fine style and I was now within ounces of my first double.

> "GROUNDBAITING HAD CLEARLY ATTRACTED FISH INTO THE SWIM - QUITE WHAT SPECIES WAS STILL TO BE IDENTIFIED"

Unfortunately, by the summer my dog food contact had left his job, (maybe too many damaged tins had fallen off the back of that lorry), but I never did try the pet food route again. I have to admit to wearing a wry smile when recently reading through the match results in Angling Times and noting the headline 'Catmeat does it again'. Apparently, the innovative anglers winning all the coin are now taking huge nets of carp on Coshida catmeat. There's nowt new in this game, gents...

Over the next few months I began to search for new venues that would enable me to finally crack the double-figure mark. That may sound so routine in this era, but back in the late '70s and early '80s it was still a weight barrier that took some beating. My attentions turned to two waters - Marbury Mere, near Whitchurch, and Osmere, just a few miles down the road. Marbury had a reputation as the kind of venue that could break a man - extremely low stocking density but a good average of fish size, if you could ever get a bite, that is.

Osmere was a different proposition, and rumour had it that bites were a little more frequent. By splitting my time between the two, I could realistically have a new personal best bream in my sights, but when I was feeling down and out, after a run of blanks, I could switch to the easier water to gain a bit of confidence. I wasn't alone in believing in the potential of these venues, and I started fishing alongside seasoned campaigners Roger Harker, Eddie Bibby, Graham Marsden and John Charlesworth - anglers with whom I nurtured a deep bond of friendship.

Osmere was a shallow water with gently sloping sides that provided very simplistic bait presentation and feeding. With a sandy bottom and no weed to ruin our rigs, it ➤

BIG FISH FROM BIG WATERS

THE SCALES DON'T LIE

"WITH THE RODS IN THE RESTS AND THE BOBBINS CLIPPED ON, WE WAITED FOR THE GIANTS TO HANG THEMSELVES…"

BREAM FISHER'S DAWN

The Cheshire meres were a focal point for big bream hunters. They were hard waters that required a lot of time and effort.

Photography www.thinkstock.co.uk

BIG FISH FROM BIG WATERS

THE SCALES DON'T LIE

allowed me to drop markers into the lake and prebait with brown crumb and maggots, then leger double maggot on a size 16 hook, to 6lb line. It couldn't have been easier.

We all caught well, averaging two fish a night - most of the bites came in darkness - but I couldn't crack a personal best, with the trophy fish scraping the 9lb mark. I felt sure that Osmere had the potential to deliver better, and I went through the groundbaiting routine in hope of better quality fish. The hours and the fish started to clock up. But my spirit was soon to be broken by a breaming virgin.

I'd turned up again on the Friday morning armed with a sack of crumb, and we were joined by a pike angler from Macclesfield who'd never caught a bream before, but thought he'd chuck his hat into the ring. Fishing from the next peg, he copied my baiting approach and cast his two rods 50 yards and proceeded to catch a brace of ten-pounders before the dawn sun had risen. I sat in the bivvy dumbstruck. What other sport could provide such beginner's luck?

My patience with Osmere was running thin, and I called time on the place after watching my bobbins dance with line bites all night only to realise the next day that Eddie Bibby had attached 2lb line to them and was under his umbrella jagging his spool of Bayer Perlon. I was up and down to those rods for hours and never got a wink of sleep. Bloody Scousers!

It was time to concentrate on Marbury, where rules and regulations meant that I had hurdles to get over and challenges to meet. The use of rowing boats was banned, so baiting up had to be done with throwing spoons, and a device that went on to be the inspiration for modern spods that are now on the market. We'd chop the top off a washing-up bottle, fill the bottom with polystyrene and attach a swivel and some heavy line to the top lip. We'd fill our bottles of Fairy with maggots, cap it with crumb and launch the whole lot into the swim.

Marbury was generally deep water, but you could find areas of 12ft, and these were spots that I focused my attention on. I fished every weekend and I hit the jackpot straight away, but not with bream. Tench after tench came to the paternostered maggot rig, but nothing prepared me for one sunny June morning in the Cattle Drink swim.

After seeing fish roll - I wasn't sure what they were at the time - I set my traps and all hell broke loose. Over the next six hours I could barely keep a rod in the water as I slipped the net under a procession of tench to 7lb 1oz. Paul Fox, pegged on the other side of the mere, even came across and gave me his maggots as I began to run out of bait. At the final count I had 43 tincas for a 200lb-plus haul - amazing sport, but no cigar... where were the bream?

As the season passed by, the tench typically melted away and by the time late July arrived there was barely a fish to be seen. It was dead. I knew Marbury was going to be a tough nut to crack, and had mentally prepared myself for hours under canvas. By the end of September we hadn't caught a single bream, and as far as we could tell, nobody else had either.

The following year during the Close Season we made lots of visits to the water hoping to spot any signs of bream patrolling or feeding, and this move proved to be invaluable. We spotted bream in three different locations many times during our visits; all we had to do now was lay the trap with a carpet of feed in any of the hot areas and catch what we'd seen.

June 16 finally arrived and Ian and I cast our baits into the swim bang on midnight, as in the

> "JUNE 16 FINALLY ARRIVED AND IAN AND I CAST OUR BAITS INTO THE SWM BANG ON MIDNIGHT, AS IN THE PREVIOUS YEAR..."

previous year. Our expectations were sky high as we had seen some tench and bream rolling over the feed the evening before.

As dawn arrived, our bobbins and bite alarms were singing as the tench arrived and, again like the previous year, we were catching plenty, many of them in the 5lb to 6lb bracket. They might not have been record breakers, but we were having great fun.

By midday the bites had stopped and the tench seemed to have moved on to pastures new. We decided that this might not be a bad thing, as at times bream don't like too much activity in their space from other species. They possibly feel bullied and often stay away from the baited area, returning to feed on the scraps of food left by the other fish. In our opinion, this was one of the main reasons bream often fed well at night.

After introducing some fresh feed into the swim in the evening, we sat back to await any pending action, and we were not disappointed. During the early hours of the morning I landed two bream, the best going 9lb 5oz - not the double that we were looking for, but at least we were up and running and the future was looking far brighter.

The rest of that summer, though, I never caught another bream. I should have gone barmy with all the boredom, but we kept our humour and still had our moments of fun. We often fished in the Cow Drink swim and whilst sitting on the fence that separated the field next door from ours, we had become very friendly with a local stallion who introduced himself by biting my arse as I sat on the stile.

We had lots of fun with this horse over the rest of the season when friends came to see ➤➤

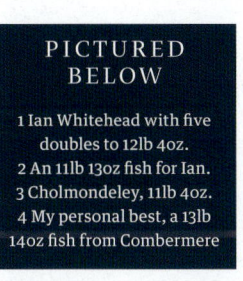

> **PICTURED BELOW**
>
> 1 Ian Whitehead with five doubles to 12lb 4oz.
> 2 An 11lb 13oz fish for Ian.
> 3 Cholmondeley, 11lb 4oz.
> 4 My personal best, a 13lb 14oz fish from Combermere

COVER STAR!

This one made the front page of the Angler's Mail! At 11lb 4oz, I was delighted and the two tone colouration makes it impossible to forget.

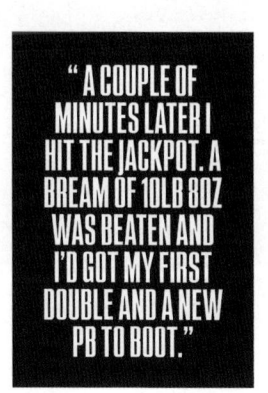

BIG FISH FROM BIG WATERS

THE SCALES DON'T LIE

us fishing. We would offer them a cup of tea and the best seat in the house on the stile, and the horse would always oblige with a bite on the backside.

The following summer we were back on Marbury again. Mini boilies had recently arrived in the shops for the first time and we decided that they would be worth a try. In the Close Season we introduced thousands of them in an attempt to draw the fish into feeding on them and, believe me, it worked... well, for the tench at least.

They went bananas on them during the opening day morning, and Ian and I caught 18 fish from 5lb to 8lb 8oz. We also watched bream rolling in the swim but, inexplicably, we caught none of them, even when we used maggots. For some unfathomable reason they just never responded.

Over the next few weeks we would see a bream or two rolling shortly after we had introduced the mini strawberry boilies. After a lot of thought, we came to the conclusion that the 'plop, plop' noise that the boilies made when landing on the water attracted the bream into the swim, but maybe the tench were using bullying tactics and keeping the bream away from feeding.

As the summer progressed, the tench, as usual, started to go off the feed and we hoped this would increase our chances of the bream feeding a little more. It was Ian who caught next, taking two over 9lb on maggot over a bed of mini boilies.

A week later, we were back on the lake for a three-night session slap bang in the middle of the hottest spell of the summer. The temperatures were hitting the mid-eighties, and as normal in these conditions, the bream were proving very difficult to catch.

As we were dismantling our bivvies to go home, a bream rolled in the swim, and a couple of minutes later my indicator rose to the butt ring of my rod, resulting in a fish of 8lb 12oz gracing the landing net. A couple of minutes later I hit the jackpot. A bream of 10lb 8oz was beaten and I'd got my first double and a new PB, to boot. Both had taken lobworm over a bed of mini boilies. Ian departed for home shaking his head in disbelief, and I stayed another night in case there were more to be caught, though sadly there wasn't.

Four summers for just six bream had left us both on the brink of insanity. It was time to move to pastures new, and we were very lucky to receive an invite to join a private mere in Cheshire called Cholmondeley. It had a low number of members, a short summer season and was about 20 acres in size. We were now in the late 1980s and early 90s and Ian and I were still keen to up our bream PBs. Going by the info we had gathered from some of the existing members, this Cheshire mere would help both of us do just that.

> "A COUPLE OF MINUTES LATER I HIT THE JACKPOT. A BREAM OF 10LB 8OZ WAS BEATEN AND I'D GOT MY FIRST DOUBLE AND A NEW PB TO BOOT."

On our first visit to the lake we were met by a giant of a bloke named 'Big' Kevin Shore. When I stood at the side of him I felt like a midget - mind you, he was Mr Cheshire, a title he was only too willing to tell you about if you had a spare five hours to waste.

I had met Kev a couple of times before, and he informed Ian and I that the timing of our membership was perfect. He explained that the bream over the past couple of years had been putting on a bit of weight, and the average had increased from 7lb to 8lb, with a few fish going up to 9lb-plus. He'd even had one of 10lb 10oz, and that beat my PB by 2oz.

Our first couple of visits to the mere proved uneventful, apart from a couple of tench of ➤

BIG FISH FROM BIG WATERS

THE SCALES DON'T LIE

PICTURED ABOVE

My good mate Ian returns an 11lb 5oz bream to Cholmondeley. We shared many a night in pursuit of these elusive giants

around 5lb. Crucially, there had been no sign of bream, but all that was about to change spectacularly on our next visit. We found them spawning in a small bay, and as we drifted over the area in the syndicate boat, there were 100 to 150 large fish. They were that busy going through the spawning ritual that they were oblivious to us, and although it's very difficult to guess the weights of fish in the water, most of them did seem to be in the 8lb to 9lb range, as Kevin had said. Plus, there were about ten further fish that stood out and were considerably bigger.

A week later, the bream had finished spawning and moved out into the main part of the mere, and Ian and I fished an area called the Wood Swims. The area was about 15ft deep and the deepest part of the mere. The swims at that time were very precarious. Two planks ran side by side out from the bank and into the mere, finishing near the deep drop-off. We had to place our bedchairs very carefully on the planks to be near to our rods, but despite our care we still rolled off our beds and into the mere.

The main reason why we chose this uncomfortable area was that on a number of occasions we had watched the bream shoal move up and down the lake patrolling the same route. On most nights we observed them in the deep area, and in the mornings they would make their way towards the shallows of the lake. As most of our fishing was done at night, the deep area was our obvious first choice.

After laying a carpet of maggots in the swim, we sat back on our chairs to await events. Ian was first off the mark, taking two fish to 9lb 6oz, and not long after that I took three fish, of 7lb 3oz, 9lb and a new PB of 11lb 4oz. These, and many others to come, were all on double maggot on a size 18 hook. On the same night,

Big Kev was fishing on the opposite bank and also had a good session, catching 17 bream to 9lb-plus.

Over the coming seasons we spent most of our weekends and occasional days in the week on the mere, often sharing fishing stories with Big Kev, Ian, Graham Marsden, John Charlesworth, Roger Harker, Eddie Bibby and a few others. They were all good anglers in the art of catching big bream. They also loved a good story, and one I would tell revolved around a still, moonless night that I spent alone in the Wood Swim.

I was suddenly woken by the loud noise of somebody, or something, walking along the planks. Frightened? I was that bloody terrified I jumped from my 'pit' and ended up in the mere! This happened on three separate occasions in an hour, and I convinced myself that the peg was haunted. Eventually I plucked up enough courage, grabbed a torch, and came face to face with… a family of badgers!

The following night I was joined by another member, Steve Redman, and the same thing happened again.

"Sod the bream, let's try to get a photo of the badgers walking the plank," I said, and we set up a camera on the pod and laid a trail of bread into the undergrowth. We both sat in the dark near the camera awaiting the badgers' return, and after three hours managed to snap the arse end of one returning to the undergrowth. I think David Attenborough's job is safe!

Over the next couple of seasons we caught plenty of bream, and as forecast by Kev, the fish were slowly increasing in weight. I had eight more double-figure fish, ➤

> " OVER THE COMING SEASONS WE SPENT MOST OF OUR WEEKENDS AND OCCASIONAL DAYS IN THE WEEK ON THE MERE SHARING FISHING STORIES "

CARVED FROM BRONZE

A beautiful example of a big bream. This one weighed 10lb 8oz - at a time when a double was a truly huge fish.

GRAVEL PIT GIANT

My good mate Rich Lee with a fish of 13lb 14oz. The goal posts with big bream have shifted in recent seasons and really big fish are a viable prospect.

but no more PBs. Ian and the lads continued to fish the mere and take advantage of these better weights, and by now there were a lot of fish being caught of around 12lb. Ian's best went 12lb 13oz, with fish eventually creeping up to nearly 14lb.

By now you might be wondering where yours truly was during those last two productive years. Well, it's like this. When a water I had been wanting to fish for many years opened its doors, the temptation was too great to miss. It was time to target Combermere, Cheshire's largest mere, at approximately 165 acres. Apart from a couple of very privileged anglers who had caught bream to 13lb, the place was virtually untouched.

On an organised day in 1994, all the members were introduced to each other and then given a guided tour of the mere on a trailer hitched to a tractor. I already knew a lot of them - the likes of Graham, Roger, Eddie and a few others. The tour also included viewing the boats that were available for use.

As a lot of the bank areas were very wooded, these boats would be invaluable in gaining easy access to areas where the fish had probably never seen a hook. After a day in one of the boats with my echo sounder I began to get a better picture of the bottom and depths of the mere, all useful info in tracking down the more likely areas to catch bream from. About 70 per cent of the mere had depths in excess of 30ft, but I managed to find a few areas of 12ft going out into the mere at varying distances, and these spots were the starting point in my quest for a new PB.

I was fishing alongside fellow member Bob Pickering one night in 1994 when Graham Marsden arrived. Like us, he agreed 12ft was a likely contour to target, and headed off 100 yards to our left in a swim that required waders to tackle. Graham needed to wade out 30 yards to make a cast, but within three steps of his

BIG FISH FROM BIG WATERS
THE SCALES DON'T LIE

casting mark his phone suddenly rang.

'Marzipan' traipsed back to the bank six times before he finally clocked Bob and I rolling around in laughter, a Nokia in my right hand. As it was, he had the last laugh by chucking his Hunters up the bank and taking to the boat to land 11 double-figure bream on waggler!

By now there had been a steady number of bream caught by members, a lot of them double-figure fish, with some going over 13lb. I, too, was now starting to catch by using the 'target bait' method, which involved a different hookbait from the bed of feed introduced. For example, I'd fish a lobworm over a bed of casters, maggots and groundbait. This approach resulted in my first few fish from Combermere, the best going 11lb 3oz - a beautiful two-tone fish and still the best-looking bream I have ever caught.

The rest of the season was a bit of a disappointment for me, with no new PB, but I wasn't too downbeat. Other members were catching the odd fish to high 13s, and I hoped it would be my turn the following year.

That next season I was back with a vengeance and was catching from the off, with fish up to 12lb falling to my rods in the first month. I had changed my approach to choosing swims, and this, coupled with the knowledge gained the year before, made me feel more confident. I noticed that most of the fish reported were being caught from the far bank of the mere, and it looked as though they patrolled from one end of the lake to the other and almost always on the far bank.

So on each visit I would enquire where the last few bream had been caught, then I would try to fish a new swim in the direction in which the bream seemed to be swimming. This new approach worked well when I finally broke my PB with a fish of 13lb 14oz on lobworm over a bed of groundbait, maggots and sweetcorn.

In 1997 my bream fishing summers came to an end for a few years when my attention was taken up fishing for large tench on another mere. I began to think that 13lb 14oz might be the biggest I'd ever catch.

But in April 2005, my close friend Richard Lee, then editor of Angling Times, rang me to tell me of a water on Northamptonshire's Bluebell Lakes complex that was doing some very large bream, and invited me to join him in pursuit of them. Old fires rekindled, I couldn't get down there quick enough.

A few days later I was there to start a four-night session with Rich and was faced with a gravel pit of approximately 20 acres, with varying depths down to 25ft. It was almost a virgin water, and very little was known about its inhabitants apart from a few carp, and a recent accidental capture of a bream and a few tench. We set up together in the same swim, a perfect, light wind blowing into our faces, and lay down a bed of bait in 12ft of water.

> "EVERYTHING LOOKED PERFECT FOR CATCHING BREAM. IN THE EARLY HOURS OF THE FIRST NIGHT RICH WAS OFF THE MARK FIRST, TAKING TWO OVER 13LB"

Everything looked perfect for catching bream. In the early hours of the first night Rich was off the mark first, taking two over 13lb, both in perfect condition and both having probably never seen a hook before.

After the second night, Rich had to go back to work, but after seeing his brace, I was going nowhere - I was determined that, even if I had to stay here for a month, I was going to catch a big fish.

It was 2am on the fourth night when one of my bite indicators finally moved up to the butt ring of my rod and the resulting bream weighed 13lb 14oz, a fish equalling my existing PB. Within minutes of returning it to the swim, my other indicator rose to signal another take, and after a brief fight, lying in my landing net was my biggest ever bream, at 14lb 3oz.

PAGE 165

TARGETING TENCH

THE SCALES DON'T LIE

IN PURSUIT OF GREEN GIANTS

PAGE 166

EARLY SEASON MAGIC

Nothing signals the start of the spring campaign like tench. I spent more hours than I care to remember chasing green giants.

TARGETING TENCH

THE SCALES DON'T LIE

PICTURED ABOVE
I still like to target tench when the opportunity arises. But the North West struggles to compete size-wise with venues in the south.

Tench are probably one of the most loved fish in Britain, and are a species that I hold in great affection. The thrill of catching your first tench and experiencing their unique fighting qualities stays with you for the rest of your life.

There have been many occasions during long bream fishing sessions when tench have saved me from going mad with boredom. They always seem to feed when other species are quiet, and once you get them going, you can catch a bagful in a session. First light to late morning has always proved to be the best time for bites on traditional lakes, but on gravel pits they can feed all day long.

Most of the Cheshire meres that I fished held a reasonable head of tench, but fish above 7lb were hard to come by. Over the years I found that the best months in which to catch the larger specimens were April, May, and June, prior to spawning.

During my many seasons of bream fishing I caught hundreds of tench, with lots weighing around 5lb to 6lb, but a friend, Ian Whitehead, and I did manage to catch some bigger fish, though. Marbury Mere produced fish to 8lb 8oz, and also a string of sevens to 7lb 10oz from Deer Park in the '80s and early '90s were the highlights.

Big tench were not easy for us northern lads to target. Unlike southern anglers, who had an abundance of rich gravel pits where the fish grew large, our pickings were relatively slim. But there is always the exception, and on a break from my bream fishing in 1995, one such water broke the mould. Barmere is a beautiful Cheshire mere located in the middle of nowhere, and it really did have it all - stunning scenery, peace and quiet and, crucially, some very large tench.

After a lot of grovelling to the small syndicate that ran Barmere at the time, I was allowed to join a very privileged group that was made up of familiar faces such as Graham Marsden, Eddie Bibby, John Charlesworth, Roger Harker and Kev Shore.

Access to the place was a nightmare, and although the walk from car to waterside was

ON THE FLOAT

Most big tench fishing requires scaled-down carp tactics but I still love catching on the float. This fish was taken on the lift method with a quill float.

TARGETING TENCH

THE SCALES DON'T LIE

short, it might as well have been a mile. Hills, bogs, long grass, fences and streams were just a few of the obstacles we had to overcome to reach the boats that were there mainly for access to the few swims that were on the mere. Making your way out of the weedbeds into open water in the boat was like a scene from the film The African Queen.

Many swims were on platforms a foot or so above the surface of the water and were not attached in any way to the bankside. In most cases they were 50 or so yards from the bank!

One of the great things about fishing Barmere were the rules - there weren't any! All that was needed from the members was common sense, and the freedom to catch fish on your own terms was a big plus. Most of the tench seemed to swim and feed along a drop-off 20 yards or so in front of the stages.

On most occasions I would arrive the night before, rake the swim if possible, then lay a bed of casters just over the drop-off. By preparing the swim, it gave the tench plenty of time to find the bait. It was a rare occasion when you had any bites before first light, but from then until late morning was by far the most productive time, and often you could watch fish rolling in your swim.

At the time, Barmere must have been one of the best tench waters in the country. Once you got to know the water it was rare that you ever blanked, and fish to 8lb-plus were almost a daily occurrence. If you were unfortunate to blank, it was normally following a heavy rainstorm that had caused both the water temperature to drop and levels around the mere to rise.

One time I was on the platform minding my own business when I noticed Big Kev had arrived to fish, and after 20 minutes or so I wondered what he was doing. I watched as he walked out into the mere carrying a number of large boulders. When I enquired what he was planning, he said very matter-of-factly that he was building a new swim so that he could fish nearer the drop-off!

He had been bringing lots of boulders to the mere for weeks in preparation, and his idea was to create his own island and then lay some timber doors on top big enough for a bivvy. Who was I to argue? Certainly not with a former Mr Cheshire!

After a few hours, a new island appeared complete with a bivvy perched on it. I couldn't believe what I was seeing! That night the heavens opened and torrential rain fell all evening. It was a poor night for fishing, and an even grimmer evening for Big Kev. Unfortunately the water had risen above the doors, and his bivvy looked as though it were floating on water. His kettle was last seen travelling downwind in the middle of the mere.

All of this had, of course, happened whilst Kev slept tightly, so I took the opportunity to awaken him from his slumbers. I bellowed down the lake, and he opened his eyes

A MAN'S BEST FRIEND

Zoe, my faithful Jack Russell, was a fishing companion of mine back in the late 1990s. Trouble was, she snored louder than me!

TARGETING TENCH

THE SCALES DON'T LIE

with a start, rolled out of his sleeping bag and straight into 2ft of cold water. I suppose it beats a traditional alarm clock!

Over the next few years, most of the members broke their tench PBs, with Graham taking the best at 11lb 4oz, while Eddie, Kev, John and Roger all took doubles. I could not quite manage those dizzy heights, but was very happy with a couple of 'nines' to 9lb 3oz, which was another personal landmark.

By the late '90s, a lot of the bream and tench in the Cheshire meres were disappearing or showing signs of weight loss. This coincided with the emergence of carp, and it seemed obvious to me that the bream and tench were suffering at the hands of more aggressive feeders. Whether that's what happened or not, trying to catch a PB tench or bream in Cheshire certainly became a lot harder.

It was in 2008 when the urge for a really big tinca returned to me, sparked when my close friend, Richard Lee, gave me a call. He told me how good the tenching had become on the gravel pits at Bluebell Lakes - the same Northants complex from which I had caught my best bream, and a place that I just loved to fish.

The complex was best known for its carp fishing, with one huge common in particular - called Benson - featuring many, many times in the angling media. It was actually voted Britain's most popular carp, and at its peak it topped 60lb. As many of the anglers predominantly fished for carp, other species such as bream and tench were, to a degree, neglected, and this allowed them to flourish on the extra food thrown into the pits by the bivvy boys.

PICTURED ABOVE

1 A five-pounder from Marbury.
2 Bivvies as they used to be! Camped up on Marbury.
3 Cholmondeley, 7lb 10oz. In those days a 'seven' was big!

PAGE 171

Rich and I have fished all of these pits regularly, and on some of the pools, weed was a major problem. Cleaning an area of weed with a rake became essential in certain spots, and proved hard work at range, so we tended to look for clearer areas before feeding heavily. Once the shoals arrived, they fed with such gusto that they did any further raking for us!

A typical initial bait menu included half a gallon of casters, half a gallon of maggots, a couple of pints of 'deads', and a few cans of sweetcorn. This was our nightly bombardment, but we'd sometimes feed again in the day if sport had been hectic and the fish had cleaned us out. When the tench arrived they would do so en masse, and the big carpet would hold them in the peg for most of the day.

Sometimes during the three or four-day sessions they would arrive quickly, and such was the number of fish, if you held the tincas ➤

LIKE THE OLD DAYS

This huge bag of tench came during a session I had on the Bluebell Complex in Northants. It was one of many 100lb-plus catches I had from the venue.

TARGETING TENCH

THE SCALES DON'T LIE

PICTURED ABOVE

Left: A big hit from Marbury when it went mad and we ran out of bait. Right: A brace topped by a tench of 9lb 14oz. Barmere was the venue.

for the duration of the trip, you'd be on the floor with physical exhaustion. The only rest from bites came in the hours of darkness, when they stopped gorging or we wound the rods in.

The place was full of tench, with the average weight being around 6lb 8oz, but a few went beyond 8lb. Some decent perch and eels also made a welcome appearance, but the carp were a little troublesome on the light gear, and could devastate your carpet of feed if they moved over it in numbers. Some of the large hauls were amazing, and there were times when we could only estimate the total weight of fish, but it certainly ran into the many hundreds of pounds.

One spring morning we did weigh the fish, after Richard offered me a challenge to catch 100lb before breakfast, which basically gave me about three hours. I did it with five minutes to spare, but I also pinched two fish from Rich's net when he went to pick up the bacon sarnies! Sorry mate, but there was twenty quid riding on it!

It was on one of the big hits in May 2009 that Lady Luck decided to smile on me. Rich and I had been battering the tench all day with fish to over 8lb and I was putting some of my tackle in my car ready for the journey home when my last rod burst into action. Just another seven-pounder was responsible – or so I thought – and I bullied it through the weedbed without thinking.

I had a three-hour journey ahead of me, and being so tired I was dreading it. I whistled Rich to do the honours with the net, and he waded out past the marginal weed to land and release it.

But Rich's reaction told me that something was amiss.

"I think I'd better bring this one back to the mat," he declared.

He waded back with the net gripped tightly between his hands, laid it on the unhooking mat and peeled the mesh apart to reveal the biggest tench I'd ever seen in my life.

Bloody hell! Just when you think you know everything about a water, it chucks up a surprise. And Bluebell Lakes has a habit of doing just that.

We put the tench on the scales and watched the dial with anticipation. At 11lb 6oz it was a fish of a lifetime, and a best that I doubt I'll ever beat.

"JUST WHEN YOU THINK YOU KNOW EVERYTHING, A WATER CHUCKS UP A SURPRISE"

AT LAST!

Having spent years pursuing a really big tench, it was ironic that my biggest should come completely out-of-the-blue. It weighed 11lb 6oz and was caught among 100lb of six and seven-pounders.

A BRUTE OF A FISH

I've always loved catfish, right back to the early days. Targeting them on the Ebro was an ambition - and this 142-pounder shows why!

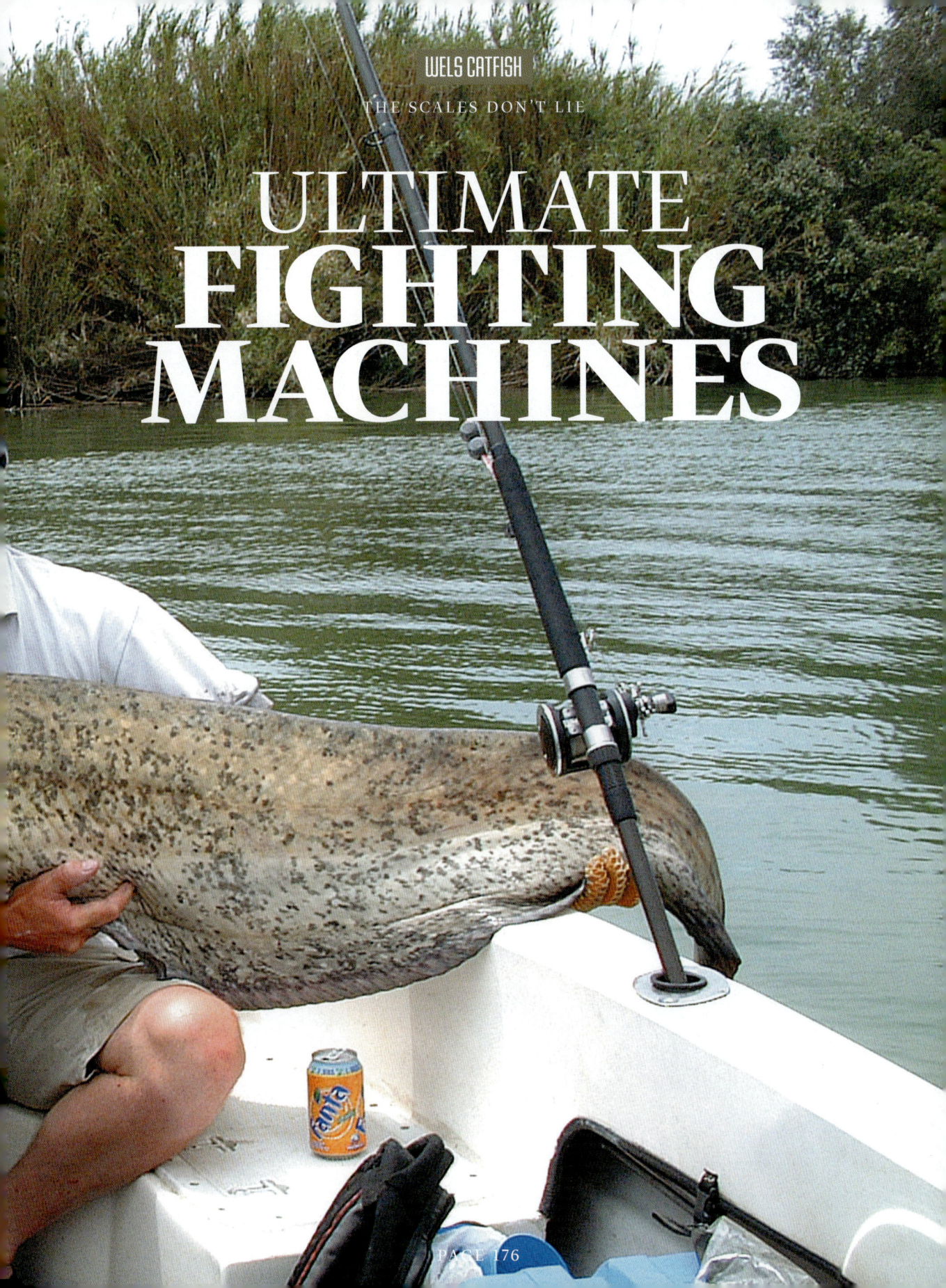

WELS CATFISH
THE SCALES DON'T LIE

ULTIMATE FIGHTING MACHINES

ALL SMILES

Rich Lee can't hide his delight at catching this impressive 100-pounder during one of our trips to the Ebro.

WELS CATFISH

THE SCALES DON'T LIE

My first encounter with wels catfish was when I stocked them into Burton Mere back in the early '90s. I looked down at 14 small fish, each no more than six inches long, swimming around the inside of a bucket, before slipping them into the mere. I remember thinking to myself that they had a lot of growing to do, but maybe one day they might just reach the dizzying heights of the monstrous predators that inhabit the now famous River Ebro, in Spain.

The main reason why I stocked them into Burton was because I am a firm believer that all waters should have a healthy population of predators. My theory was that species such as pike, perch and cats would feed first on any dead or weak fish in the lakes, the end result being that the rest of my stocks would become a lot stronger and also a lot healthier. I did have some concerns that if the catfish grew significantly in size, they would eventually eat most of my silverfish, but over the years the opposite seemed to happen.

My stocks did indeed became healthier and continued to increase in numbers and size, so much so that every year I was now selling unwanted fish to fishing clubs and raising much needed income for the fishery.

Catfishing in the UK was also becoming more popular, anglers' appetite for catching large specimens growing by the week. Over the next few years I learned a lot about the cats. They were, in my eyes, both a great scavenger and a phenomenal predator. I found that one of the best baits to catch them on was the largest cube of luncheon meat I could attach to a hair-rig. They absolutely loved it! They were certainly aided in finding the meat and other food sources by their unique and very sensitive whiskers.

My first fishing adventure involving big cats came when I was on a carp trip to France. My main target was proving difficult to catch, so I decided on a change of direction and to have a go for one of the cats that also inhabited the lake, which reputedly had been caught in excess of 80lb. After a quick visit to the local supermarket, I managed to buy a box of fresh squid, which I was told was a favourite bait amongst hardened cat anglers and certainly worth a try.

> **WAITING GAME**
>
> Fishing for cats requires specialist gear....and a specialist approach. The rods await a massive drop back that signals a take.

IN ON THE ACT

My other half, Chris, enjoys her fishing and this 85lb Ebro cat provided her with a proper scrap.

PAGE 179

WELS CATFISH

THE SCALES DON'T LIE

Just before dark, my three rods were all baited with squid and cast into the lake. I was then joined by Rich Lee, Graham Marsden, Eddie Bibby and a few others for what can only be described as party time. These meetings had, over the years, turned into a bit of a ritual. We would often sit there into the early hours talking about fishing, politics and many other topics, and we were always indulging in the delights of French wine and cuisine purchased from the local supermarket. I don't normally drink when I'm fishing, but with the very good weather and all of us enjoying the holiday atmosphere, I do make the exception in France.

I should have smelt a rat because Graham and Eddie were not known for their generosity when it came to giving away their wine. To put it another way, they were normally as tight as a duck's arse! The two or three glasses that they had already given me were very good, and I was by now well on my way to being very merry.

"What do you think of the wine, Tel?" asked Graham.

"Very good," I answered. "Another would go down very well."

But, unknown to me they had swapped the good wine for a cheap gallon container full of what I can only describe as rocket fuel. I hadn't noticed, and by 1am I was so drunk, all I could think about was getting my head down. The only problem was, when I tried to walk to my bivvy, my legs wouldn't respond and I kept falling over! It seemed to take an eternity to

PICTURED ABOVE
Heading out for a day's catting on Spain's River Ebro. The venue has become a Mecca for big cat hunters in the last 20 years.

reach my temporary base, and it seemed to be getting further away when it should have been getting closer.

I was properly drunk, and it was only thanks to Rich's help that I finally made it over the last couple of metres, finally falling into bed and going out like a light.

I'm not sure how much later it was when I woke up to the sound of a strange noise, which at first I couldn't identify. Bloody hell! It was my bite alarm! I fell out of my bivvy and landed on all fours, staggering to my feet in a state of confusion. It's amazing how quickly you sober up with the sound of a bite alarm going off, and I was soon at the rod, pulling the hook home into my first catfish.

Rich then joined me (he seemed to be the only one who wasn't suffering from the previous night's excesses!), mainly to check that I was okay to land the fish. After assuring him that I was fine, I went on to bank a fish of 38lb. I was well pleased, and certainly wanted more of the same. Another one of 25lb followed a night later, the other lads taking fish in excess of 50lb.

My next experience with cats came when I was back in my office at Burton Mere. My bailiff at the time, Alan Bassnet, burst into the office to inform me that he'd just caught two 20lb fish that he wanted my help to photograph. Alan was trying hard to hold the two at the same time for a brace shot, but was struggling to get them in the correct position.

"Hold on," I said, putting the camera on the ground before moving towards the fish in order to help get the shot set up correctly.

As I steadied myself to grab one of the cats, it suddenly, and very aggressively, bit my fingers. I staggered backwards in complete disbelief.

"Bloody hell! The bastard just bit me," I shouted, struggling to get my head around what had just happened.

This was a real shock to my system, and although it didn't hurt, it certainly frightened the life out of me. Up to that point I had never been bitten by any fish before.

However, these prehistoric fish were really beginning to pull my string, not just because of their size and power, but also because the methods required to catch them were very similar to my favourite fish, the pike. Being able to target cats in summer, when pike were strictly reserved for winter, was a real plus.

Our next catfishing trip took us to a venue near Metz, in France, called Chalet Lake. Although our main quarry was carp, we always carried our spare gear so that we could have a go for the cats. The week was another success. The pensioners on the trip, Graham and Eddie, couldn't stand the cold, so one night, in their search for warmth, they ended up in the lake lodge, where they could build a nice fire in the lounge and fish from the walkway outside. The problem was, they'd forgotten that the lodge was built on stilts, and the walkway was approximately 8ft above the surface of the water. I was fishing about 100 metres away when I was awoken in the early hours by noise from their direction.

I was soon at the lodge, and what greeted me was a scene that resembled something from Dad's Army - Graham as Captain Mainwaring and Eddy being Corporal Jones! The two OAPs were having all sorts of problems. Graham was playing a cat in the 50lb-plus range from the walkway, while Eddy was trying his hardest to land it for him, the flaw in the plan being that Eddy's landing net pole was 2ft too short, and to make matters worse both of their head-torches had packed up!

After making them promise to supply me with two bottles of decent wine, I agreed to help and was soon lying on the walkway floor, leaning over the side, with Eddy holding onto both my legs. Fortunately, I soon had the fish, and all three of us lifted it to safety, where it was weighed in at 56lb - a new PB for Graham.

Over the next few visits to the water we all caught decent cats, and my PB went up to 38lb 8oz, and latterly 51lb. Chalet Lake provided us with some superb fishing, with excellent carp and grass carp fishing adding to the enjoyment. We enjoyed the freedom of being able to fish where we wanted, and because there were very few rules, it felt extremely comfortable, and trips were always a pleasure.

> "BUT MY DRIVE TO CATCH LARGER CATS WAS GROWING BY THE DAY. I JUST HAD TO CATCH SOME REALLY BIG ONES, SO RICH SUGGESTED FRANCE..."

But my drive to catch larger cats was growing by the day. I just had to catch some really big ones, so Rich suggested we could benefit by employing the services of a guide, or someone who knew the waters in France well. We still wanted the option to fish for carp, but also have the opportunity to target big cats.

In truth, we didn't have to look far. Luke Moffatt had been appearing in the fishing magazines for a number of years, and as Rich was at the time editor of Angling Times, he was soon able to make contact with Luke. A week's fishing on the River Saone, near Lyon, was quickly booked, and I couldn't wait - his guiding service had produced a number of fish well in excess of 100lb-plus, which were exactly the size we were after.

We were joined on the trip by our friends John Wakelin and Kevin McLean, and the group decided that one day we would fish in pairs from the boat, and the next on the bank for carp. We'd simply alternate from one day to the next. After the toss of a coin, Rich and I had the pleasure of targeting the cats first, and it became very clear why Luke was rated so highly as a guide - he knew the river like the back of his hand.

He told us the venue had been fishing well, and the best method to catch the cats was to drift downriver with suspended live eels fished under the largest floats I had ever seen. We had to present the baits just off the bottom of the river bed, and the best way to do this was with an incredible method that involved holding the braided line between two fingers and watching the echo sounder. You'd simply lower the bait if the depth increased, or lift it up if it got shallower, all the time monitoring the echo sounder for a visible sign of a huge cat coming of the bottom. If they were fished too close to the bottom they would find any snags, resulting in lost fishing gear.

While Rich and I would be holding the rods and keeping a close eye on the echo sounder, Luke controlled the shape of the boat with an electric motor, ensuring that we drifted downriver at the right angles. He would also employ the use of a clonk, which is an unusual tool capable of attracting catfish. When the clonk is being hit correctly in the water, it creates an air bubble that, with proper movement of the hand, makes a deep sound that I can only describe as being similar to the opening a bottle of wine. Catfish are territorial predators who jealously defend their space, and the sound produced by the clonk stimulates their defensive instinct. Essentially, it makes them ➤

PICTURED BELOW

The business end of a big cat. They are powerful creatures with huge mouths well capable of taking big baits.

WELS CATFISH

THE SCALES DON'T LIE

PICTURED ABOVE
1 Using a net to catch livebaits is a real skill.
2 Taking the strain as 100lb of pure muscle attempts to evade capture.

more aggressive, encouraging them to attack any fish in the vicinity. Luke had certainly mastered the use of the clonk, but when Rich and I had a go, we got soaked pretty much every time… much to Luke's amusement!

It was on our first drift downstream that Luke shouted to Rich to look out. A fish had shown up on the echo sounder screen, and almost immediately it took the bait, pulling the braid out of Rich's fingers as it surged away. A fish of 35lb was soon beaten, and although it wasn't a monster, we were up and running. As it transpired, our group had around 40 fish, the best being a new PB to Rich at 64lb. I had my fair share, but no new best.

The experience of fishing with Luke provided us with plenty of instruction. He certainly knew the river well, was equipped with the right tackle and knew how to use the echo sounder and clonk. What we'd picked up was bound to help us in our future search for bigger fish. Something else that we learned from Luke was what not to do with our eel livebaits.

On one of the days when Rich and I were on the boat, the fishing was a little quiet. Luke decided to make the time pass a bit quicker with what he described as his party piece. At the time I thought he was about to sing to us, but he turned his back, started fumbling into the livebait bucket and, while Rich and I looked at each wondering what was going on, he turned around to face us. Well, I nearly fell out of the boat! He had two eels hanging by their teeth from the end of his nose, and was shouting: "Look, no hands!"

The eels were wriggling like hell, but with their teeth still firmly embedded in his hooter, they weren't going anywhere. I was rolling around the boat laughing my bloody head off, when Luke asked me if I fancied a go.

"Get bloody stuffed," I remember saying in a flash!

It really was one of the funniest moments of my life, and one I will never forget.

Within a year, Luke had purchased his own carp lake in France and named it The Graviers. I was one of the first to book this new water, and on one of the trips I was again in the company of Rich Lee and Kevin McLean, while the fourth member of the party was Steve Broad. Rich suggested we split the week's carp fishing into two, and have three days after the cats on the Saone, with the remainder of the time carping on The Graviers. Steve didn't fancy it and was willing to look after our carp tackle while we headed off in search of predators. We were soon on our way further south towards Lyon to fish the Saone, and Luke took us to a ➤

PICTURED BELOW

He might not look it, but my good mate Dave Flynn (left) was chuffed with this beautiful-looking Ebro cat.

swim he called 'The Pipe', where he had caught many cats in the past.

The weather was steaming hot. Temperatures were around 100 Fahrenheit and there was no boat to fish from this time, as it was bank fishing only. Live fish were again the preferred choice of bait, but these were fastened to marker buoys, which is a tactic favoured by hardened catfish anglers. We were well eager to try it for ourselves.

With the use of a small boat we placed our markers, which were made from one gallon plastic containers, in the swim. These markers were then fixed by a rope to a heavyweight anchor. Attached to these was a 6ft weak link of 8lb line that ends in a swivel fixed to the braided reel line. We'd then tighten down the rod tip and place the butt in a metal pipe that we'd hammered into the ground. This left the rod in the full vertical position, with the tip bent well over and taking the strain of the marker. The whole idea of the method is to keep the livebait just under the surface of the water, and with the line taught, it helps reduce the chances of any tangles from the swimming bait. When the cat takes the bait, the 8lb line breaks, causing the rod tip to bounce violently backwards, shaking the bell that's fixed to it to indicate a bite.

This trip wasn't the most productive we have had, but we managed a couple of fish, Rich taking one of 30lb-plus, while I broke my PB with a cat going 74lb.

Within a year, the draw of the River Ebro had become too much to resist. There were increasing reports in the press of large cats being caught, and some of my friends at Burton Mere had been over to Spain to enjoy the 'Ebro Experience', returning with fish in excess of 100lb under their belts. These lads had been using the guiding services of Alan Henderson and Martin Fawcett and they came highly recommended. According to the Burton lads, there were no better guides on the river.

Their services were mainly carried out in the lower reaches of the river, where there was little bank fishing and angling activity was a lot quieter. From 2003 to 2008 we visited as often as we possibly could, even taking our wives with us. Al and Mart would pick us lads up from the hotel at 8am, dropping us back at 6pm. Eight hours' fishing in a day was plenty in the hot sun, and while we were away, the girls would visit the local beaches or lounge around by the pool.

On one of the trips my wife, Chris, and I decided we'd head out to Spain ten days earlier than the rest of the group, so we could enjoy some holiday time together. The plan was to meet up with the angling crew (plus wives) on the Ebro in the second week. This seemed like a good idea at the time, until on our second day of sightseeing in the beautiful city of Tortosa, we nearly met with disaster.

> "I WAS LEFT TO ACT OUT THE ROLE OF MY EVERTON HERO, DUNCAN FERGUSON... BUT SECONDS LATER I WAS ON THE FLOOR IN AGONY. MY KNEE HAD GONE"

I had been continually telling Chris to watch out for the traffic, with speeding cars and narrow streets making for a dangerous combination. However, within minutes of my latest warning, a car came far too close for comfort, and when I shouted for Chris to jump out of the way, she moved with a start and landed awkwardly on her ankle. It immediately began to swell up like a balloon, and she laid the blame squarely on me - if I hadn't have shouted, she said, she'd never have fallen awkwardly. Typical. Sometimes us fellas can't do right for doing wrong!

A visit to the local hospital confirmed a very bad sprain, and at least a week's rest, together with crutches, was prescribed by local doctors.

"Bloody hell!" I thought. "What a crap start to our sightseeing trip."

At this point it looked like most of the coming

week was going to be spent in and around the hotel.

The next day we were sitting around the pool, Chris resting her leg as much as she could, and me reading a book. But I soon became bored. It was then that I spotted a lad kicking a ball around just across from us, and I just couldn't resist the temptation to have a go.

After a bit of persuasion, the young lad agreed to go in goal, and I was left to act out the role of one of my Everton heroes, Duncan Ferguson. Two shots and two goals later, I was now on a real high, a crowd of 40,000 ringing in my ears. They wanted a hat-trick, and I was not going to disappoint them. I struck the ball one more time, a sweet right-foot drive that looked destined for the top corner... but the little sod saved it!

I didn't have time to dwell on my near miss because within a second I was on the floor writhing in agony. My right knee had gone. After a visit to hospital, I discovered that I had torn my cartilage. My football days were officially at an end.

"You silly old sod," said Chris... numerous times.

I couldn't argue, and with both of us on crutches, we looked a right pair. Over the next week we tried our hardest to get fit, occasionally visiting the local bar to drown our sorrows, but by the time the fishing came around, I was still pretty sore. Rich and Kev McLean, though, were on hand to help, and I managed to climb into the boat for our first day's catting.

What I liked most at this time on the Ebro was that there were few restrictions on the use of livebaits. With the use of a throw net, we could always catch mullet, and sometimes small carp, and the supply was plentiful.

Another reason why I enjoyed it was because the methods used for catching the cats were in many ways very similar to those employed for targeting my favourite species - pike. Yes, ▸▸

BIG AND BEAUTIFUL

Another Ebro 100-pounder. I know many anglers don't like cats, but for a self-confessed predator lover, I think they present a fantastic challenge.

WELS CATFISH
THE SCALES DON'T LIE

the gear was much stronger, but the principle was the same. A free-running livebait presented under a float and fished off the back of a boat is the ultimate method for catching all predators, and cats are no different. The floats were very large, but they needed to be. When baits are in the 2lb or 3lb range, you need something extremely buoyant, and these were the size of pint milk bottles!

Al and Martin would guide the boat down the margins, using the electric engine to control the angle of the vessel and allowing us to fish our baits in the flow of the river 40 yards downstream ahead of us. The big plus with this method was that the baits would pass through new areas that we hoped held cats well before the boat came through. When we got a take, Al or Martin would immediately start the petrol engine and stick it in reverse, pulling the fish out of the margins to avoid any potential snags.

The only problem with this was that if the fish were big, our thumbs, which were applied to the spool of the multiplier to slow down the run of the fish, would burn like hell with the friction.

On our first couple of trips to the Ebro I couldn't believe how many cats seemed to inhabit the river. On many of the drifts downstream we would see fish of varying sizes splashing their tails on the surface, sometimes causing our boat to rock with the force. On one occasion we fished the river just after the spawning season had finished. I can only describe the condition of the cats as horrendous: they were covered in cuts and scratches, and some had fresh blood pouring from open wounds. I was later informed that during their sexual activity, the cats would regularly bite each other, and that their wounds would soon heal completely.

Their diet was another eye-opener. Just after landing some of our fish, they would often regurgitate what they had recently eaten. On the menu were fish, crayfish, snakes and, on one occasion, a whole egret! I would imagine that the RSPB would not be very pleased about that.

PICTURED BELOW

Big fish require proper tackle and you can't afford to take on Ebro catfish without it. Big floats are used to suspend big livebaits.

This part of my fishing life provided some of the most memorable experiences I could wish for. The catfish really pulled my string, and their prehistoric looks and awesome fighting qualities will remain with me forever. Over the years we fished on the Ebro we had many a cat over 100lb, and we caught fish from shallow, fast water, deep, slow water, snags and clear swims, and they would always put up incredible scraps.

My PB rocketed to 142lb, with another six over 100lb. Rich had fish to 118lb, Kevin to 100lb-plus and Dave Flynn had them to 111lb. My 142-pounder nearly saw me off. As I was fighting the fish, our captain for the day, Martin, decided it would be better to weigh it in the boat. He began to prepare the sling, which was made with two 9ft poles connected to some PVC material, by lying it along the floor of the boat. He then proceeded to throw a bucket of water over it to prevent any damaged being caused to the fish.

By now I thought I had beaten my fish. It was close to the front of the boat and looked tired, so Martin decided to grab it by the jaw to haul it over the side. However, the cat had other ideas! It shot off like an Exocet missile, dragging me along the full length of the wet PVC sling and almost over the back of the boat! If Rich hadn't grabbed my belt I would have been swimming in the river alongside the fish!

Martin's next attempt was more successful, and the impressive creature was soon lying on the sling. It looked well over 8ft long, and to say that I was pleased would be an understatement.

I can only say that Ebro catfishing is truly awesome, and if you have never done it, try it, and soon, because I hear these fabulous fish are under increasing threat from many different sources.

What I would say, though, is that over here in the UK serious controls on stocking are needed, and I believe that catfish should not be introduced into any of our wild rivers. However, I am sure that commercial-type enclosed venues similar to Burton Mere would be ideal. Trust me, no other freshwater fish on these isles pulls back like the catfish.

PICTURED ABOVE

1 Playing big cats is a tiring affair...especially when you're in your 60s!
2 This 73lb 8oz cat came from the bank during a visit to France.

ASIAN ADVENTURES

THE SCALES DON'T LIE

The lake WHERE DREAMS ARE MADE

ONE BIG MOUTH!

The siamese carp at Gillhams fight like stink and when they grow to over 100lb, it takes its toll!

PAGE 189

Catching exotic fish such as Mekong catfish, Siamese carp, Amazon redtail catfish, arapaima and many other different species had long been a dream of mine.

To do battle with huge fish - some of which grow to enormous sizes - was something I became keener and keener to do, and thanks to the age of technology, I was able to finally realise that goal.

My destination was Gillhams Fishing resort in Krabi, Thailand, and accompanying me were long-term angling friends 'Big' Kev Shore and Dave Flynn.

Owned and managed by Stuart Gillham, a respected angler himself, the complex had become internationally recognised as the ultimate big-fish venue, with Stuart's experience and knowledge helping to create something very special indeed.

On arrival, a walk around the lake confirmed what the three of us had hoped for - this was a place where dreams really could come true! We saw enormous fish roll - some 8ft in length - and set in stunning surroundings, it really did feel like a piece of fishing heaven.

But what really makes Gillhams such a superb location is that the accommodation is 5 Star, with the addition of a swimming pool that ensures the wives and girlfriends are kept happy while the boys get on with the important business of catching giants!

We were introduced to the two guides who work at the fishery - Mat The Yank and Chubby Scott. Mat was to be our guide for the week, and it was his job to advise us on the best ways to catch the fish, along with helping with all unhooking procedures, fish care, taking photos and numerous other jobs.

> "TO DO BATTLE WITH HUGE FISH - SOME OF WHICH GROW TO ENORMOUS SIZES - WAS SOMETHING I BECAME KEENER AND KEENER TO DO"

I have to say that I was a little mindful. The wildlife that inhabits this part of Thailand includes king cobras, tree vipers, scorpions, massive spiders and other aggressive looking creepy crawlies. But Mat put my mind at ease, assuring me that although they do get occasional visits from some nasties, these encounters are rare occurrences.

Most of the super-sized fishing tackle is supplied by the fishery - and it's not for the faint-hearted! You get three Free Spirit Cat Tamer rods with test curves of 6lb, and three Shimano Long Cast Baitrunner reels, one loaded with 100lb braid for predators and two loaded with 36lb GLT Pro Tough for general carp fishing. With 47 different species, 15 of them to World record size, this type of tackle might be heavy, but it's essential.

Mat informed us that the three main methods of catching fish were 'Baggin' Waggler', Method feeder and a slow-sinking bubble float with a fish as bait for the predators The daily supply of bait consisted of groundbait, maize, fish bait similar to sprats, and boilies if you required them.

We soon got in our swims for the week and the adventure was about to begin in earnest. The anticipation was high, and with many different species of fish still rolling in parts of the lake, together with patches of feeding bubbles that resembled Jacuzzis, we were itching to go.

It wasn't long before Kev, who was in a swim to my left, shouted "Fish on!" and blew the whistle we had all been given to alert the closest angler to reel in and prevent any crossed lines. It turned out to be a Siamese carp of 40lb that fought like hell all the way to the waiting net. We all stood around looking amazed at the size of the mouth on the fish, and it became very obvious that ➤

ASIAN ADVENTURES
THE SCALES DON'T LIE

to keep them feeding in the swim we'd need a lot of bait. These things were like vacuum cleaners!

That first day turned out to be Kevin's best of the week, his next whistle-blowing moment coming later in the evening when he was up to his neck in the water and passing through mine and David's swim!

His face was as white as a sheet and he was shouting as line screamed from his Baitrunner at an incredible rate of knots. What he had hooked was clearly very large and it had dragged him at least 150 yards and was still going, heading to the bottom corner of the lake at the speed of an express train

I thought to myself that Kev is one big lad at 6ft tall and about 17 stone - how would someone my size cope in a similar situation? The mind boggled.

One hour later the fish was in the landing net and a much-relieved Kev, despite having a bad back, was left to cradle a Mekong catfish that took the scales down to an eye-watering 150lb. It had taken two grains of hair-rigged maize and after witnessing the power of that fish I could not argue with our guide, who said the Mekongs were probably the hardest-fighting freshwater fish on the planet. Big Kev enjoyed every minute of it. He even managed to add another later in the week at 120lb.

In an attempt to keep the fish feeding, over the next few days we bombarded the swims with lots of free food. Kev and I fed up to 250 big groundbait balls and 20kg of maize each, the latter taken out by Mat ➤

> **ONE BIG MOUTH!**
> The siamese carp at Gillhams fight like stink and when they grow to over 100lb, it takes its toll!

PAGE 191

> "HIS FACE WAS WHITE AS A SHEET AND HE WAS SHOUTING AS LINE SCREAMED FROM HIS BAITRUNNER AT AN INCREDIBLE RATE OF KNOTS"

ASIAN ADVENTURES

THE SCALES DON'T LIE

in the boat and spread around the baited area. Dave, meanwhile, approached it in a similar manner, but with boilies instead.

The fishing time was limited from 7am to 6pm, but the constant temperature of 32 C made everything we did feel like hard work. But the effort was beginning to pay off. Fish of a variety of different species were now showing up. David was blowing his whistle fairly regularly as he caught Siamese carp to 55lb and lots of redtail cats to 56lb. Big Kev had Siamese carp to 40lb and redtails to 60lb, while I was catching Siamese carp to 50lb and small redtail cats.

However, the last day of the trip was to be mine. After watching Kev playing his Mekong cats, I really wanted to live the experience, and by midday the Jacuzzi effect was happening in my swim. The vacuum cleaners had arrived, and there seemed to be a few of them.

I knew this was last chance saloon. Minutes later all hell broke loose as my left-hand rod burst into action. My God! The fish ran 200 yards in the blink of an eye and almost hit the far bank before I'd had a chance to react. The fight was unbelievable and although I genuinely feared being pulled into the water, there was no way that I was going to let go of my rod. My feet were firmly on the ground and the clutch was going to have to do its job.

Forty long and hard minutes later the fish was in the net and I had got the biggest smile imaginable. It wasn't as heavy as Kev's, but at 85lb it was big enough for me and I was absolutely delighted.

This was the first serious fishing trip to the Far East that any of our group had enjoyed,

PICTURED ABOVE

1 Kev Shore and his 110lb stingray.
2 Gillhams - a special place.
3 50lb redtail catfish
4 A 28lb pacu.

PAGE 193

ASIAN ADVENTURES
THE SCALES DON'T LIE

and we loved every minute. You could spend a lifetime trying to catch any one of these species in their wild environment, with time and money needed in equal measure. Yes, Stuart Gillham has created a commercial fishery, but it's one that is probably the finest of its kind anywhere in the world. That first trip had been a good one, but it had been a learning curve and we were all convinced that we could enjoy even better sport next time.

January 2012 came around fast enough and Kev and I, with wives in tow, were back in Thailand and eager to get back among the big fish. We agreed a plan of attack that involved both of us feeding our chosen swims heavily with pellets. We also decided to rotate swims every day, just in case one was better than the other.

When you fish at Gillhams you are allocated a number of 30mm pellets and some deadbaits for predators. These are supplied on a daily basis, but you can purchase more bait, so we got two 20-kilo bags of pellets most days to keep the fish occupied in our swims. We also had two new guides - Joel and Little Stephen - and by the end of the week both of them came to know Kev and me very well. We made their life hell at times with the banter but, joking apart, they were great guys who couldn't do enough to help us.

The fishing was hectic, and from the start the Mekong were running riot. These fish just didn't know when to give in, and would often run to the far end of the lake - a distance of approximately 200 to 250 metres, depending on the swim being fished. The other anglers on the lake were often ➤➤

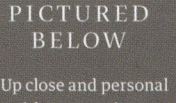

> **PICTURED BELOW**
>
> 7 Up close and personal with an arapaima.
> 8 X marks the spot! The buggers sprayed me with dye as I played a fish
> 9 Rods set - the wait begins.

ASIAN ADVENTURES
THE SCALES DON'T LIE

A THREE MAN JOB!

Holding an arapaima, especially one as big as this, is no mean feat. 180lb of pure muscle and anger!

forced to bring their rods in to avoid any crossed lines and to lessen the chance of tangles, which could result in lost fish.

We were coaxing the fish all the way back to our pegs, and then they would simply decide they didn't like it there and away they would go again! There wasn't much you could do about it except play the fish on the clutch and be very, very patient. Most fish would take up to 90 minutes to land, while others would run for the cover of weedbeds that grow along the edges of the lake, and they could be a real pain at times.

To avoid any chance of losing fish in weedbeds, anglers can jump into the lake and keep the rod tip low in the water, applying lots of side pressure to gently ease the fish into open water. The only problem with this is that if you are a 'short arse' like me, and the fish has a tantrum, you find yourself being dragged into deep water! Big Kev saved me on a number of occasions by jumping in and holding me under my arms to keep my head above water!

After the first few days I was a physical wreck. I was what they call 'Mekong-ed Out' after catching ten, of which eight were over 100lb. My best went 175lb, and I'd had enough! Big Kev was also 'Mekong-ed Out'. He too managed ten, his best going 155lb.

Our attention was now being focussed on the other large and exotic species that inhabit this fabulous water. A change of swims was in order, and by fishing the margins on the far bank, it gave us a chance of keeping away from the Mekongs, and giving the other species a chance to taste the delights of our hair-rigged 30mm pellets.

ASIAN ADVENTURES
THE SCALES DON'T LIE

It soon became obvious that the change of swims and approach was going to pay off, and we were soon into fish. The pellet rods were doing well, and we were starting to catch a variety of different species, such as Siamese carp, Asian and Amazon redtail catfish, and nut-eating pacu from the Amazon.

We never had any idea what we were going to catch next, and over the next few days I managed to take: six Siamese carp from 32lb to 65lb; four Asian redtail catfish from 1lb to 15lb; ten Amazon redtails from 18lb to 50lb; and pacu of 22lb and 28lb. Kevin's results were very similar, and the fishing was, in our view, World class. But, incredibly, the best was yet to come...

The arapaima in the lake are known to weigh well in excess of 400lb, and at nearly 10ft long, these fish provide a truly awesome battle if, indeed, the angler is lucky enough to hook one. Noted for being hard to tempt, they might show themselves regularly when they roll on the surface to take gulps of air (unlike other fish that take oxygen from the water, the arapaima takes it in from the surface every 20 to 30 minutes), but hooking one is another matter entirely.

One regularly used method involves the use of a bubble float loaded with some water so that it sinks very slowly, bait normally being a dead fish. When you spot an arapaima taking air, the idea is to cast just in front of its head in the hope that the fish spots it dropping slowly through the water.

But getting a take is only half the story. The bony nature of the arapaima's mouth, coupled with the ferocity of its head-shakes when hooked, can make it a very frustrating experience. But, boy if your hook does hold, you're in for the fight of your life!

They often thrash on the surface of the lake, or try to dive or smash their way through the weedbeds as they attempt to shake the hook loose. And the sight of one of these massive fish trying to dislodge the hook is frightening, and even dangerous. They have a reputation for being capable of seriously injuring some of their captors, largely because they can leap high into the air in an attempt to escape, and if you're in their way, a bad injury to your head or upper body could result in a visit to the local A&E department!

When it comes to landing these massive fish, the use of the guides is essential. They use large holding cages that are placed in the water, and when the fish is close enough, they carefully guide it in. Then, with the arapaima secure, they carefully remove the hook, and when it has recovered from the ordeal, the captor can then stand between the two guides and all three lift the fish gently onto the surface of the water for photographs.

> "TO AVOID ANY CHANCE OF LOSING FISH IN WEEDBEDS, ANGLERS CAN JUMP INTO THE LAKE AND KEEP THE ROD TIP LOW IN THE WATER"

Returning them is also a fraught affair that requires great care. Standing well back, the guides tip the cage onto its side, allowing the fish to swim away. But sometimes things don't go to plan...

On one occasion, one of my fish - a specimen of 180lb - that we thought was safely in the cage, decided otherwise! As the guide tried to remove the hook, it shot off like a missile! It went straight through the end of the netted cage, leaving a gaping hole in the middle, and headed way back out into the main lake at a rate of knots!

Luckily the Baitrunner on the reel was on, allowing the fish to take line, and we were able to quickly pass the rod though the

ASIAN ADVENTURES

THE SCALES DON'T LIE

PAGE 197

ASIAN ADVENTURES

THE SCALES DON'T LIE

door of the cage and out of the hole, and I was able to keep in contact with it. Not long after that we safely landed, unhooked and photographed it, but it just went to show what volatile creatures arapaima are. We all took a deep breath, grateful that none of us had been injured and that the fish was able to fight another day.

The weather in this part of the World is something else. It's stinking hot for most of the time, then in a matter of minutes it can completely change, with awesome thunder and lightning displays preceding truly torrential rain. When I say that it can soak you to the skin in moments, I'm not exaggerating. But then the sun will reappear and within half an hour it'll be blazing hot again! It's in these conditions that you have to be on your guard. It acts like a trigger to the fish, and for a short while they go feeding mad, sending your confidence sky high.

During these periods you need to stay firmly focused on your rods, as you await the impending action, and the adrenaline really starts to course through your veins. It was in exactly these conditions that Big Kev - who became known as The Big Fairy largely because of all his grunting and groaning whenever he was playing fish - hooked his first very large arapaima. As I arrived at his swim to help out, I found him up to his neck in water.

"What the hell have I hooked here?" he asked, in between groans.

"That's a man's fish!" I replied, just as it decided to surface 250 metres down the lake.

The guides were shouting at him to add side pressure by plunging the rod tip under the water. This can help prevent the fish going airborne and shaking the hook loose. After about an hour, and with The Big Fairy now utterly exhausted, the guides had it safely in the cage. It was a cracker at 280lb, but the jammy sod had another at 340lb shortly afterwards.

It wasn't long before it was my turn to do battle with another seriously angry arapaima. Only this time I was determined to beat it on my terms. There was to be no jumping into the water - I wanted to get this one in from the bank.

In an attempt to make it a bit easier, I decided to sit down at the front of my swim. However, unbeknown to me I was showing what it is commonly know as a 'Builder's Bum', and it was only when I felt something between my cheeks that I realised that the guides behind me had sprayed a blue cross between my arse crack!

Now this is stuff they use to treat any open wounds on damaged fish, and although painless, it is semi-permanent! They were rolling around with laughter behind me, but I was still determined that all of the micky-taking wouldn't put me off, and I was going to land the fish from the bank. Well, after 60 minutes of semi-torture and a blue backside, we finally got her in the cage, and at 220lb she was a new personal best. I was in Seventh Heaven, and even my blue cross backside wasn't going to get me down... even if it was still there three weeks later!

On the last day of our trip, The Big Fairy decided to change the bait on his predator rod. After rooting around in the bait tub, he decided to give the chicken's liver a go.

"What do you reckon, Tel?" he asked.

"Good bait, but it might give you a fish you don't really want to catch."

"Like what?" he asked.

"Just you wait and see," I said.

With about an hour of the final day to go, The Big Fairy's bite alarm sounded as a ➤

> **PICTURED LEFT**
>
> This siamese carp could well have been a new personal best - but it escaped the scales and gave me a soaking, too!

ASIAN ADVENTURES
THE SCALES DON'T LIE

PICTURED ABOVE
My old mate Dave Flynn takes to the water to stay in touch with a Gillhams giant, while Kev Shore (far left) helps out.

slow but steady run materialised. But just as he got to the rod, silence. He picked up the rod, cursed under his breath and wound down to something completely solid - whatever had taken the bait had run into a snag. He continued to add pressure, and a few minutes later it was on the move.

"Bloody hell, it's heavy," he shouted.

At this point he had no idea what was on the other end. Minutes later it stopped dead again.

"Come on, keep the pressure on it," I laughed. "I'm pretty sure I know what it is and you need to get it off the bottom."

The Big Fairy looked at me puzzled. I couldn't keep it to myself any longer.

"It's a stingray! Just keep as much pressure on the rod as possible and it will come up, I promise you."

After another ten minutes it was on the move, but a further quarter of an hour went by and while it may have been only four metres in front of the swim, it was still stuck hard on the bottom.

"Bloody hell, I'm fed up with this!" shouted The Big Fairy,

"I told you it was a fish you wouldn't want to catch!" I replied, laughing as I did so.

Not long after, Shaun, the owner's son, arrived at the scene and confirmed that it was indeed a stingray. He offered to get into the water to try to coax it off the bottom, something he'd done successfully before for other anglers who had almost been beaten into submission by the fight. He also told us that for health and safety reasons the stings from each of the resident rays had been removed when they'd been stocked.

Shaun entered the water and was soon diving into the depths of the lake looking for the fish that had anchored itself firmly, and seemingly immovably, on the deck. It seemed he'd been gone for an age (and with no breathing apparatus) when suddenly his foot rose above the surface and began shaking violently.

"Bloody hell!" I shouted. "He must be in trouble!"

But before we could do anything, the foot disappeared and we all looked at each other wondering what on earth was going on. Then, without warning, he popped up on the surface and started giving us an almighty bollocking

"UNBEKNOWN TO US, HE'D FOUND THE STINGRAY, GRABBED IT BY THE TAIL AND PULLED IT LOOSE..."

WEIRD AND WONDERFU

These wallago attu are might not be the best looking of fish but they fight like stink. The grip ensures no nasty bites!

for not grabbing his leg! Unbeknown to us, he'd found the stingray, grabbed it by the tail and managed to pull it loose. If we'd got hold of his foot, we could have pulled the pair of them up and given The Big Fairy the chance to play the fish in open water.

Bollocking duly administered, and with us now aware of what needed to be done, we got in position. By this time the other bailiffs – Joel and Little Stephen – had arrived and the three of us were in the water forming a human chain that ended with The Big Fairy. Shaun went under again, and when his arm appeared a few moments later, Joel grabbed it and together we heaved backwards.

Within the space of a few seconds we were all - including the 110lb stingray - lying in a heap on the bank laughing our bloody heads off. It truly was one of the funniest moments of my life, made even funnier when The Big Fairy dusted himself down, took one look at the fish and said:

"Sod that! I don't ever want another one of them!"

THE ASIAN FISH HAUL

MY FISH FOR THE WEEK

Siamese carp: 35lb, 44lb, 32lb, 28lb, 32lb, 65lb;
Asian redtail catfish: 1lb, 7lb, 14lb, 15lb;
Mekong catfish: 100lb, 165lb ,110lb, 100lb, 120lb, 100lb, 85lb, 110lb, 85lb, 100lb, 175lb;
Amazon redtail catfish: 18lb, 17lb, 18lb, 50lb, 35lb, 18lb, 25lb, 22lb, 25lb, 22lb; **Pacu:** 22lb, 28lb; **Arapaima:** 220lb, 180lb.

KEVIN'S FISH

Siamese carp: 32lb, 35lb, 38lb, 45lb, 45lb;
Amazon redtail cats: 12lb, 15lb, 15lb, 15lb, 18lb, 18lb, 18lb, 20lb, 20lb, 20lb, 20lb, 20lb, 22lb, 23lb, 25lb, 25lb, 25lb, 25lb, 25lb, 25lb, 25lb, 30lb, 35lb, 40lb, 50lb, 55lb, 65lb;
Asian redtail cats: 15lb, 7lb, 2lb; **Sorubim catfish:** 20lb, 23lb;
Stingray: 110lb; **Arapaima:** 280lb, 340lb;
Mekong catfish: 80lb, 90lb, 80lb, 90lb, 100lb, 115lb, 100lb, 125lb, 130lb, 155lb.

ASIAN ADVENTURES
THE SCALES DON'T LIE

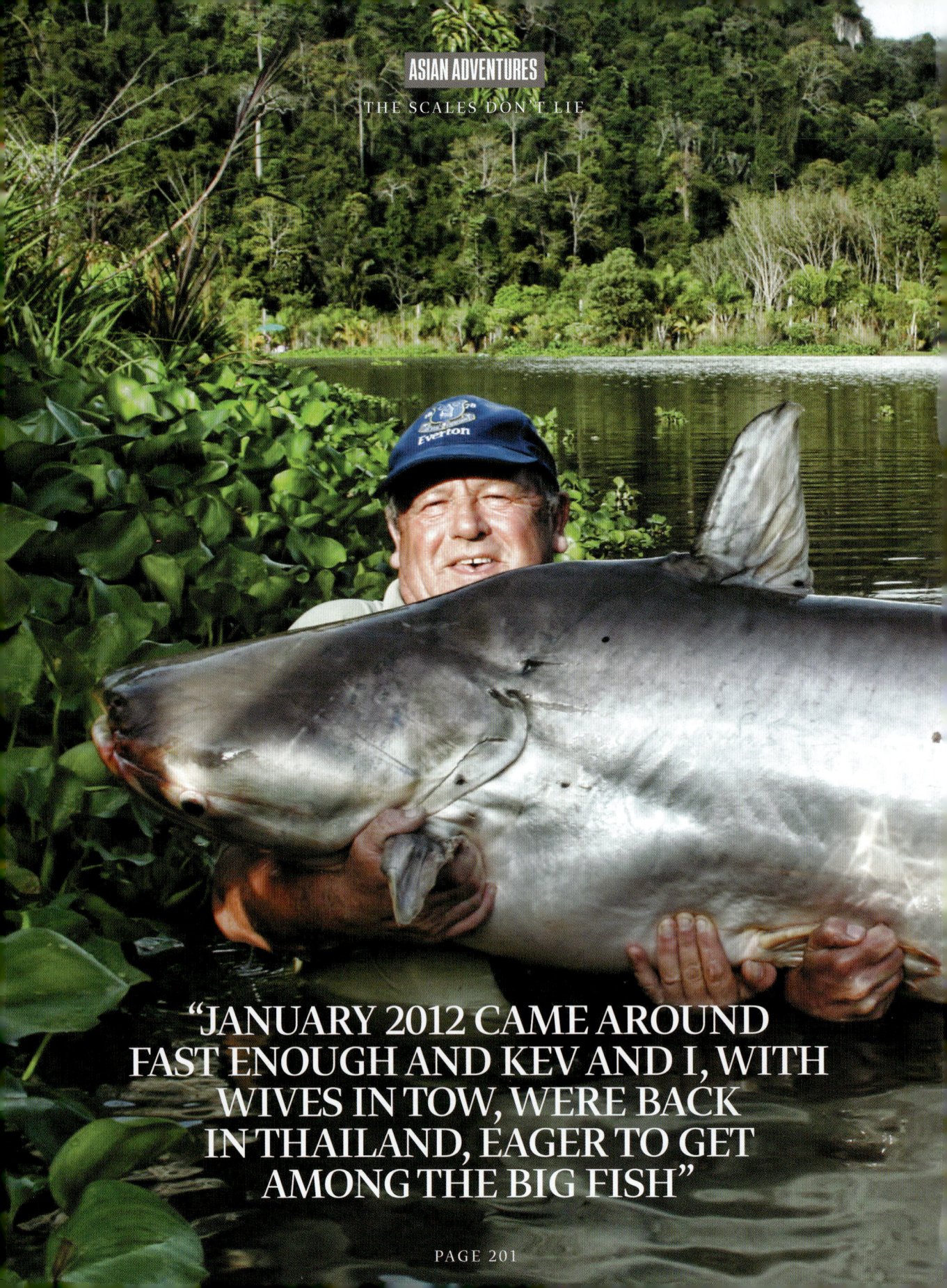

"JANUARY 2012 CAME AROUND FAST ENOUGH AND KEV AND I, WITH WIVES IN TOW, WERE BACK IN THAILAND, EAGER TO GET AMONG THE BIG FISH"